UGLY MONEY, FAIR MONEY

To the memory of my mother Arati Das who taught me to think straight

SUDIP KUMAR DAS

1st Edition November, 2018

Copyright Sudip Kumar Das

Cover designed by Gourab Das

UGLY MONEY, FAIR MONEY

Contents

Foreword   ..   ..   i-iv

Chapter 1 : Usage and Paradigm – the Match-making   1

Chapter 2 : Anatomy of Pricing -
               Compensation & Skewed Propriety   11

Chapter 3 : Money - Yardstick to Measure Compensation   17

Chapter 4 : Money –
               Menace of Toxicity in Over-Accumulation   29

Chapter 5 : Mobility Profile of Money - Trans-cycle Accumulation
by Growth, Savings, Interest, Intermediation and Investment   45

Chapter 6 : Beacons of Pricing Evolution –
               Quiddity, Monery and Normey   53

Chapter 7 : Ugly Money, Fair Money   69

Chapter 8 : Money-making Marks –
               Bias, Cast, Drift, Edge and Hyperform   77

Chapter 9 : Money-making – How it Warps the Minds   83

Chapter 10 : Normey –
               Fair Visage of Money, Vehicle of People's Dream   93

Preface

This writing is the result of the writer's inspired intention of a maiden foray into authorship on the one hand and presenting, on the other, a few posers to readers, many of whom may have been kindly indulgent out of curiosity to know with what temerity an unknown author might be mooting a subject that is otherwise overlooked, sidelined and branded as lacking enough merit to engage valuable attention of the intelligentsia at large.

What the author likes to convey through this writing are ideas born out of ordinary observations of a common man rather than stingless erudite rehash of recondite pre-formed notions. If a small idea has the power to pierce and deflate an enormous balloon, why not let the balloon be deflated and get replaced by more efficient transport? When we all have miles to go why not go all the way where our own unbridles ideas take us to. Our thinking process need a new lease of life, undeterred by the prospect of losing prodigious possessions that may have been occupying the space meant for ideas - for too long and too strongly with their staid, dressed up anachronisms and hidden flaws. The fear of leaving large voids could be unnerving but turning a void into useful creative space is mind's work. If we allow the minds to do their work in synchrony, there is no greater force in the world.

The author is peddler of a small idea. All he wishes is to see the sapling that he plants in his readers' minds grow boundlessly. The author truly hopes that a tiny idea has been successfully put across and in best of lights. Contributions of my son, Gourab, are immense and critical at once, for he worked both the cover and the technical niceties. But for Amazon's fabulous support this book would not have taken off at all.

UGLY MONEY, FAIR MONEY

Foreword

Aspiration is a wild duck. Its flying habits that is, the way simmering aspiration is vented out from within oneself gets one painted to oneself and to outsiders too. It all depends how much liberty the wild duck gets. If one tries to contain it within the contours of conventional wisdom it becomes a dead duck – mindless and sterile in its lifeless existence. If one allows it to take to wings without minding the habitat then it might travel to unknown lands and may make a new habitat there for all others to follow. A free-flying wild duck not necessarily achieves a lot in life. Mostly it does not achieve anything at all. Neither does it get anything from its peers except derision for holding contra views. That does not stop it from seeking the new lands that lie far, far away – beautiful, green lands where yellow sands play with blue waters. This writing embodies a lively wild duck.

Like the wild duck one can be innately vivacious if one has the freedom of choice in self-application. A society without rigueur of dogma is almost non-existent. Dogma enslaves minds. Capitalists too are dogmatic in their deliberately indifferent treatment of labour as mere commodity in the market, not caring to consider labour as a part of the productive enterprise entitling it to a share in the gains gleaned out of production. By extension, this disdain percolates down to people who produce labour to vitiate their mindset. Deprivation of labour is thematic to enrichment of Capitalists and a dogma key to creation of economic classes and ceaseless class conflicts. To be able to see things in the light of clarity one has to sideline dogmas.

This writing holds no pretensions as to being an exposition on Economics, concerning itself more with ways of looking at Economics rather than Economics itself. It scans for niche space for itself to dwell the dividing walls between Economics and Dialectics on one hand and Economics and Political Economy on the other. In this rigmarole, Money emerges as the key figure since, unless Money is clearly understood, rest of Economics degenerates into inchoateness. Money is ageless mystique that enraptures and invades deep into inner psyche where questions of ego, security and self-propagation loom. The entire cross-section of humanity at all ages have been subject to its charm. Yet Money has thwarted many a dream, catapulted many an undeserved to great heights and reduced even the highly deserving to dust. Money, by design, lends unabashed support to opportunists, bullies and their flunkeys including talents. In the process, Money destroys values.

As time advances new themes and ideas emerge to add freshness to life in ceaseless iterations. Even these sparkling and exciting insertions to life cannot stop erosion of values because hope and values run contrary to each other. The upshot is angst, that grips our distraught minds with an all-pervasive dichotomy. The world would conceivably be a different place to live in if hope and values supported each other. Hope from new discoveries counterbalances distress from deterioration of values. In this milieu, only people uncaring of values are comfortable. Sadly, this genre gathers force with time. We aim to draw alternative parallel design for Money where values are protected but, at the same time, leave the extant form of Money intact.

A question frequently asked in the context of Money-making is "Is it a crime to become rich"? The question has much more depth to it than is apparent. The answer is "No, unless what you have begotten has no involvement of opportunism, bullying or selling your talent to bullies". Who has ever become rich without resorting to opportunistic practices, bullying or, demeaning himself as a crony of the bully? Capitalism ensures that one does not.

This writing attempts to draw a line between Money and Money-making while presenting a parallel to Money capable of exposing real worth of the vile horde of campaigners of Money-making. Its Usage makes Money irreplaceable but its parallel has implications deeper than Money - allowing for the compulsive and incisive charm that it has - promising to unify many a sensible mind in a common logical thread. As the writing unfolds, the reasons to have a parallel to shadow Money become apparent. The author only hopes that his reasoning is clear and acceptable to his readers.

Data finds use here as aid to illustration and to bringing out logical streak underlying the data. Here, maintaining sanctity of historical facts is priority. Diversion from focus, if any, is unintended. Historical baggage is off-loaded. To use a simile. Opening a book on Anthropology while probing a human body to pinpoint area of affliction for its root cause and treatment - is regarded as insane. We basically look for parameters that track motions of Money, its genesis and accumulation. In the process, inadequacies of Money come to the fore to inspire further thinking on redress.

P.iv

The term "Capitalism" is very frequently invoked, implying genuine full-fledged Capitalist form of production as well as those systems which are merely market for goods produced by Capitalist economies but which themselves have adopted Capitalism to a limited extent are included in its purview. The word "Capitalist" has an enlarged implication - it includes owners of production machinery, managers of the show and supporters.

The word "cycle", often used here, is more of an allusion to an imagery where all production-cycles are assumed to be concurrent and are of same duration. It aides assimilation with its simplified platform and, despite its own absurdity, does not rob concepts of their applicability.

The term "Pricing" has an extraordinary connotation here. It points exclusively to ratio-formulation mechanism with which exploits of production is dispersed among Capitalist, labour and agriculturist. This bargaining for sharing of gains has no arbiter and, as such, is an arena where lawless tussle prevails.

This writing gazes out beyond confines of rigid and staid texted Economics and breathes in fresh air sweeping across free-thinking space. Where it touches Economics it does not enter the large garden of many floral varieties in bloom. It takes intense peeks at one tiny part of the garden though. It is Money - to which we direct our focus entirely. Money is not above social forces, nor is Economy. Money, ever-changing under evolution, is seen as tending to approach a point of no-disparity with fairness in firm control of all aspects of Economy.

UGLY MONEY, FAIR MONEY

Chapter ~ 1 ~

Usage and Paradigm : The Match-making

Money is mainly known for its many uses and a long history. We do not find these relevant when we try to dig deep into Money itself. Outlandish though it seems, we use Money not knowing what it really is. Our limited familiarity with Money ends at the crucible of Usage. There, Money forms an amorphous mix with a cluster of mystified real-life entities namely, systems, institutions, faiths, beliefs and ethos that control our lives.

Hard to understand, Money has two distinct personas - Usage and Paradigm. Usage is familiar, Paradigm is not. Usage is Money in circulation. Paradigm is abstraction of facts gleaned out of it, explaining phenomena with constructs. In order to know Money we have to reconcile these two personas and bring them under fold of a single entity, knowing that erection of an all-weather bridge joining the two sides, entrenching into firm ground, failed efforts of two centuries allowing floating bridges, which tremble under impact of big waves and disintegrate in storm, to stay ineluctable.

Money is the face of Pricing – the nerve-centre of Capitalist system. Money is ugly because Pricing is the gene-like code - a sordid one- of Capitalist system. Part of anatomy of Capitalist system - Pricing to be exact - is our focus. The anatomy, like that of all living things, undergoes evolution. Evolution of Pricing is an area with a vast expanse, tracking down of which reveals a great deal about a particular segment of history of mankind since about 1815 when modern Money was born and Capitalism was just fledgling and taking shape. But first we sort out rift between Usage and Paradigm.

We know Usage of Money. About role of Money in a Paradigm we are unaware. A Paradigm has an ingenious conceptual core around which theories are super-built. The yarn that weaves such intricate fabric is Money. A logically precise core averts elaborate cover of mathematics and laws of physics. In a three-way dynamics among man, production exploits and human relations the last one - born out of conflict over share in exploits – is our angle of vision.

Why do we need a Paradigm at all? Paradigm gives the edge for keener insight into the Capitalist system that matures, morphs and is stricken with pitfalls and crises oftener – phenomena which would be inexplicable otherwise. An acceptable Paradigm must have inbuilt ability to : (1)Explain events of Economics (2)Stimulate and guide progress (3)Predict, prepare for and avert systemic crises (4)Uphold human values (5)Foster Nature conservation. We only generate leads necessary to build Paradigm perfectly.

Is Paradigm feasible without palpable, apt contours of Money? No. Usage-specific efficacy of Money may be lost in its grafted form in Paradigm, the abstraction. Concept of God is a case in point where idols worshipped by Stone-Age people preceded ubiquitous God. They lack compatibility.

Before probing the element Money, we examine Flagstones, the building-blocks, which are intermediary modules made up of Money-play that, assembled together, can form Paradigm. Flagstones are conceptual modules from real-life performance pattern of economy.

P.4

Flagstones Srl	Symbol	Real World Equivalent	Flagstone Class/Id		[Table-I Type
01	F_s (*)	Skill/Scholarship	Pro	Bg_2	Bargaining
02	F_u	Upper Kernel (more in Table-3)	Con	Cn_2	Consuming
03	F_c (*)	Capacity	Pro	Ad_2	Aiding
04	F_k	Kernel (more in Table-2)	Con	Cn_1	Consuming
05	F_i	Investment	Pro	Ad_1	Aiding
06	F_n	Nature/Device/ Exit/Medio/Cash	Con	Cn_3	Consuming
07	F_g	Gold	Neu	Dn_1	Neutral
08	F_m	Manpower/ Innovation	Pro	Bg_1	Bargaining
09	F_y	Yellow-page Entry/Nature	Pro	Ad_3	Aiding
10	F_t	Tilling-land	Pro	Ad_4	Aiding
11	F_h	Housing/ Housing-Land	Neu	Dn_2	Neutral

Kernel : Consumption Originating at Roots Level

[Table-2]

Srl	Code	Category	Implication
01	K_r	Ration	Food is the most basic need
02	K_p	Protection	Self-preservation is overpowering
03	K_f	Family	Procreation/mating are natural
04	K_h	Health	Medical attention essential to life
05	K_d	Dwelling	Basic cover against the elements
06	K_s	Sustenance	Continuity of life's process
07	K_c	Community	Social togetherness gives strength.
08	K_e	Entertainment	Flexing of mind with diversions
09	K_l	Literacy/Training	Basic step to higher mental goals
10	K_o	Occupation	Need of mind seeking refinement
11	K_a	Aspiration	Need of mind seeking glory

Upper Kernel : Consumption Related to Framework

Srl	Code	Category	Implication	[Table-3
01	U_a	Administration	Enforcement of Law and order	
02	U_d	Defence	Resistance to external aggression	
03	U_i	Infrastructure	Conveyance, communication etc	
04	U_j	Job creation	Scope for earning a livelihood	
05	U_o	Opportunity	Opening for aspiring people	
06	U_r	Recognition/ Leadership	Facility for talents to blossom	
07	U_s	Social norms	Control on behavioural extremes	
08	U_t	Trends/Ethos	Changes in tandem with tradition	
09	U_b	Brand image	Influencing minds, mainly young	
10	U_e	Environment	Sensitization on surroundings	
11	U_g	Govt machinery	The Govt has its own baggage	

Table-1 above lists out Flagstone types while Table-2 elaborates on consumers, without particular attention to whom study of Money is pointless. Table-3 has exclusive consumers, mostly institutional. Among these three namely, F_u, F_k and F_n are from Consuming (Con) section while six namely, F_s, F_c, F_i, F_m, F_y, and F_t are in Providing (Pro) section with two namely, F_g and F_h form Neutral (Neu) section.

The ConS represents the consuming urge of which need is a part and the rest is need-plus. The ProS represents the supplying compulsion or providing of which production is a part - the rest is production-plus. The NeuS represents facilitator role - similar to that of a chemical solvent - of which money is a part, the rest is money-plus.

Money starts with Nature and ends with Nature. ProS supplies while ConS absorbs. ProS is the creator of Money. If ProS is immediate cause then ConS is actual *raison d'etre* of ProS as well as of Money. Thus, ConS is the real driver.

Growing population, although natural, adds complexities to human relations, enlarging and widening ConS. So, ProS constantly needs to gear itself up to cope with the ever rising and occasionally ebbing thirst of ConS. Innovation and system resilience are biggest supports here.

The real task of building a Paradigm lies in stitching these Flagstones together to form a single entity that is, the economy. Here, unlike in a necklace where beads combining together in a string are inert, every Flagstone need to sync with every other Flagstone in dynamically.

P.8

```
              |-------------------|
Providing ---→|   Facilitating    |-----→ Consuming
              |-------------------|



Production ---------→|
                     |--------→   Providing
Production-plus --→|



Need -------------→|
                   |--------→   Consuming
Need-plus ---------→|



Money -------------→|
                    |--------→ Facilitating
Money-plus -------→ |
```

P.9

Providing is cyclic by nature. To make the scenario less complex, we may assume that everyone is contributing to Providing – some more, some less. For someone contributing more, it is human nature to demand a token recognition of this fact. Even in this simplified scenario, such demand throws up multiple questions none of which has a simple answer but actually leads to diverse ramifications aptly summed up as human relations. Human relations is an area where questions of principle invariably crop up.

q1. How to recognize individual contributions to wealth growth?
a1. (Suggested lead) Pricing!

q2. How to quantify recognized differences of contribution?
a2. (Suggested lead) Money!

q3. How to keep tag of consolidated quantification across cycles?
a3. (Suggested lead) Growth!

These questions relate to prosperity of people and, by extension, to human relations too. The suggested leads need elaboration. A direct approach can develop the leads into Paradigm using Flagstones as modules but that is beyond our scope for the elaborateness of it. We have alternative less and complex methods at our disposal which we will try out in the remaining part of this writing. Those are indirect approaches but can take us very close to reality with application of pragmatic assumptions and approximations. We exit this method at this stage with the offer of leads.

P.10

Instead, we take a detour. We accept conventional wisdom as our starting point and morph it, enlarge its scope with introduction of new angles of vision while we adapt it to reality. Thus we are lead indirectly to a version of Money that is fit for Paradigm and in complete sync with a highly responsive human relations matrix made up of prosperity, equitability and homogeneity as elements.

UGLY MONEY, FAIR MONEY

CHAPTER ~ 2 ~

Anatomy of Pricing : Compensation with Skewed Propriety

Prosperity expresses itself in terms of Money. Conventional wisdom on Money starts with Production and includes Pricing. In a simile, Pricing spins raw cotton, or goods, into yarn, or Money, which in turn is woven into fabric, or economy. Pricing, a code and basic discerning mode for contributions to prosperity, is bedrock of human relations among groups called classes. The question of rights out of contribution to prosperity which Pricing settles, is one of propriety too that needs mooting of issues of Value, Wealth and Labour.

Value is what all cherish. It is either Intrinsic or Usage. To amassers of wealth Usage Value is par with Wealth which all try to earn and accumulate. Owners of production apparatus are self-appointed as sole creators of Usage Value, sidelining Labour. Such bias warps attitudes, thought processes and human relations. Labour, thus forced to pair up with Agriculture as input, tradable in commodity Market at a Rate of Exchange (RoE), or, Usage Value, is debased.

Capitalism sees labour as an essential prerequisite to production as much as inputs are. But, labour is treated as external to the process of production itself - where settlement of labour's dues is concerned - an arrangement in terms of which labour loses the right to a claim in the proceeds of sale of goods after production. Labour's dues are settled without reference to sale proceeds but only against work done in producing goods. There is no set formula but constant bargaining. This is core of Capitalism and crux of Pricing where altruism is precious but often taken amiss.

P.13

Sale proceeds of goods minus cost of labour and inputs is fresh wealth created. After sale of goods, key role shifts from RoE to Pricing. Prati, functional face of Pricing, equals RoE and splits into (a)labour or Humanity in Toil (HiT), (b)materials or Other Inputs to Production (OIP) and (c)owner or Means of Production (MoP). Selling of goods done, Pricing takes over lead role through Prati.

Prati (P) ------
(= RoE)

| ---- Prati of work by HiT (P_a)
| ---- Prati of OIP including agro (P_b)
| ---- Prati of enterprise by MoP (P_c)

$$P = P_a + P_b + P_c$$
$$f_a + f_b + f_c = 1 \qquad [\, f_a = P_a/P,\ f_b = P_b/P,\ f_c = P_c/P \,]$$

Where f_a, f_b and f_c are a set of fractions. Managing f_a, f_b, and f_c is so arduous a task that it becomes a test of ingenuity for pundits at negotiating difficult terrains - often uncharted too - and critically important for prosperity. Owners of MoP demand steep price for enterprise enacted by MoP. HiT resists such attempts. MoP, by virtue of their ownership of production set-up, dominate and twist Pricing to win but not without endless conflict.

This is also dispersal mechanism for spoils of fresh wealth created in production to reach the hands of HiT and OIP engaged in generating buying power. By denying HiT and OIP their dues - using political clout - MoP actually makes buyers of their own goods shrink, inviting crises. Constant preemptive moderation of Pricing defuses crises.

P.14

The origin of wealth disparity lies in the splitting process. Prati is never split equitably by MoP. Different mechanisms have been explored - some with State intervention - to bring in a semblance of equitability in the splitting process, one of which is Socialism.

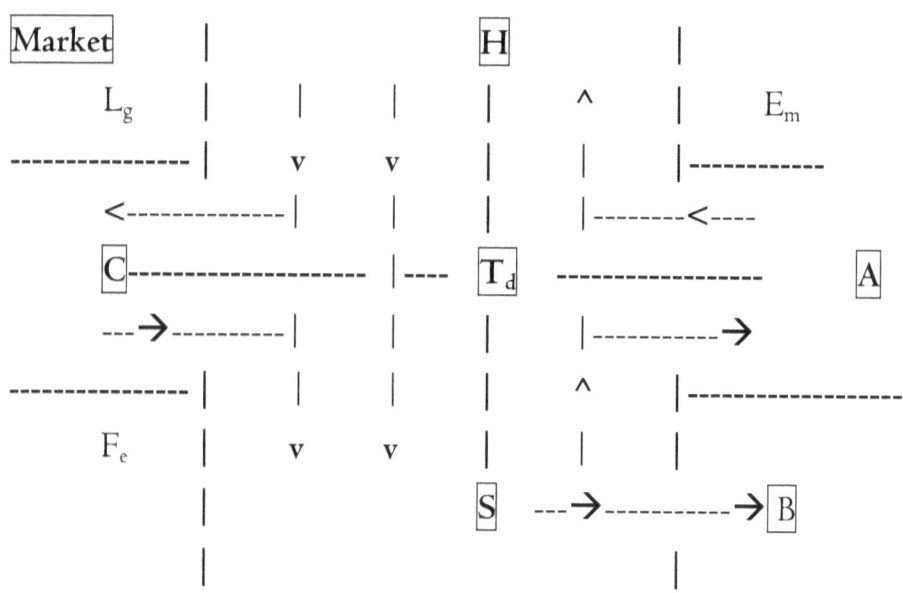

In Market, the platform, Table-top T_d rests on C-A-S-H, the legs;
C = Capacity, A = Agriculture, S = Service, H = Humanity-in-Toil;
T_d = Trade, B-E_m-L_g-F_e is a buffer between T_d and C-A-S-H;
B = Inert-Capital-B, E_m = Employment, L_g = Logistics, F_e = Finance.

$^\wedge C_p = Z_a(H-C) - Z_a(C-S)$ [Z_a is down-stream flow of Wage increase

$^\wedge B_p = Z_a(H-S) - (Z_a(S-A) - Z_a(C-S))$ [^ indicates growth
$^\wedge A_p = Z_a(S-A) - Z_a(A-H)$ [subscript p indicates product source
$^\wedge C_p + ^\wedge B_p + ^\wedge A_p = Z_a(H-C) + Z_a(H-S) - Z_a(A-H) = ^\wedge W_g.$

P.15

$\wedge W_g$ is rise in Wages from C, A and S. As earning from Agri Toil $Z_a(A-H)$ is static, contest is direct between $Z_a(H-C)$ and $Z_a(H-S)$ for share of $\wedge W_g$. Thus, when wages rise, $\wedge B_p$ intercepts to eat into $\wedge C_p$. As $\wedge W_g$ is key to Money generation, $\wedge C_p$. We have,

$$(\wedge C_p/\wedge W_g) + (\wedge B_p/\wedge W_g) - (\wedge A_p/\wedge W_g) = 1$$

where, $\wedge C_p/\wedge W_g$ is Increase in consumption of goods as well as Increase in Money creation as Ratio of and in consequence of Increase in Wages from all sources. Till this ratio – Market Force for Wage Settlement (MFWS) - stays positive in the margin, Wages go on rising as Money creation is boosted by it.

So, the pertinent point here is that, increase in Wages is not decided on merit of the Wage earners but by self-interest of the Capitalists. MFWS limits to increase in Wages, not Wages in the absolute sense.

With A neutral, spurt in sale of goods, $\wedge C_p$, depends on successful prevention of $\wedge W_g$ from being lured away to B. In general, $\wedge B_p > \wedge C_p$. So, a point comes in an Economy – the Critical Point - when $\wedge B_p$ equals $\wedge C_p$. As B enlarges, its pull on W_g increases to sink $\wedge C_p$.

Rate of Exchange (RoE) can play a crucial role in this regard. With the aid of technology, RoE of goods can be brought down while quality can be improved. These two factors in tandem push up $\wedge C_p$. As $\wedge B_p$ relies more on mind-play than anything else, conflict between B and C is not head-on. It is rather complex.

Rate of Exchange (RoE) connects Pricing to Market. Market is the place — notional or real — where bargaining takes place to arrive at a RoE acceptable to both sides engaged in the bargaining. How RoE crystallizes depends not only on the demand and supply matrix, product quality and discernibility but also on issues of compulsive nature such as fear of impending scarcity. The totality of all these factors is called Market Force.

In the preceding context, a very important economic category is introduced to the picture — the buyer or, the consumer. Buyer's taste can be a decisive Market Force.

How much a consumer earns, out of which how much he spends and how much he saves for the Bank and for investment — these are questions that are ultimately decisive in fixing the prosperity scenario of an economy. Unless the consumer buys, products will remain unsold and factories will shut down because fresh products are no longer wanted since unsold goods use up the entire space. Unless the consumer saves, there will be no investment and again the factories will shut down for want of Money. So, it is the consumer who keeps the factory running. Who takes care of the consumer's earnings? It is Pricing which plays this key role and determines how affordability is handed down to the employees and wage-earners that is, the HiT who, as group, form the fountain-head of demand in the economy as they are also the principal consumers of goods. So, the direction an economy takes depends much on the Pricing policy it adopts. As such, if consumer affordability is reverse side of a coin, its obverse is wages.

UGLY MONEY, FAIR MONEY

CHAPTER ~ 3 ~

Money, the Yardstick that Measures Compensation

Wages and consumer affordability are two sides of the same coin that is minted by Pricing, a dirty game of which Money is the seedy outcome. The dirt is made invisible as it is swept under the carpet artfully and religiously so that only the beauty of the carpet is left to be seen and appreciated.

We will desist from getting rid of either entirely though from a pragmatic point of view because of their deep-rooted Usage utility. We will look at certain modifiable aspects of Pricing in due course. Pricing and compensation formula find expression in wielding of the hoary yardstick, Money, that turns Production gain into market reality. To consummate its role-play as shaper-fixer of wealth dispersion Pricing needs appurtenance of a unit. Money fulfills that part while mooting the subject of Ownership.

```
                    |---Ownership of Source of Manpower (OSM)
     Ownership ---|
                    |---Ownership of Means of Production (OMP)
```

Both Owner of Source of Manpower (OSM) and Owner of Means of Production (OMP) are easily identified but ownership of the net gains from Production is fiercely debated. Money, the arbitrary yardstick to measure net gain from Production, after all dues of Manpower and Inputs have been met, is not above dispute. Neither Manpower nor Agriculture has exclusive yardstick of their own but are quoted only in a supporting, subjugated role vis-à-vis Means of Production. The yardstick of Money is forced onto both Manpower and Agriculture.

If Pricing is the chevalier who sways to the tune of pragmatism, then Money is his dance companion. The most potent economic entity, Pricing, is incomplete without Money. Money conveys what Pricing has to express.

In trying to answer relative contributions subtle distinction between Reward and Compensation needs to be examined for contributions to production. While Reward is readily relatable to Stake holding there is a stumbling block called investment that separates Compensation from Stake. That is, once production is over, those who contributed labour to make such product possible are delinked from the product by mere payment of Compensation as per arrived Formula. Thus, Stake of OSM in the product is unrecognized in Capitalist system. Instead, OSM's contribution is related to an abstraction called Money. This detachment of OSM from the fruits of efforts with intervention of an accounting jugglery is a characteristic feature of the Capitalist system. This forced detachment divides society into classes, sowing the seeds of disparity and class conflict too. Expectedly, the Formula is artificial, contrived and unfair as also heavily biased in a way that leave a wide scope for Reward to capture the lion's share on discharging of its dues to OSM with mere payment of Compensation.

Classes as well as Money did exist in the Feudal system too but those were qualitatively and intrinsically different from those in Capitalist system. The concept of wages as being reward for labour related to the work done to create the produce but unrelated to the proceeds that the produce actually fetched – remains the same. Quantum of produce did not decide fresh generation of Money in the system though.

Criterion-wise, dividing line between the Ruling Class and the Ruled Class in the two systems of production revolves around the mode of discharging of OSM's dues by OMPs in respect of output generated. In the Feudal system the discharging was effected post-production, mostly materially as a portion of the crop. Money was neither a prerequisite nor of absolute relevance in the process of settling the dues of OSM. In the Capitalist system, such discharging is enacted essentially through use of an accumulation of carried down value called Money. Hence, Money is an integral part of production accounting on which the Capitalist system stands and absolutely relevant to it.

In fact, Capitalist Money or Modern Money derives its definition from the transaction mechanism of settling the dues of OSM in production process. Thus, in this concept, richness is an abstraction residing in accounting books, unrelated to tonnage of holding of precious metals. Also, Modern Money and currency in circulation are not synonymous. By contrast, Antiquated Money in use in the Feudal system was in principle equal to currency in circulation and was entirely related to volumes of precious metals held in the custody of the respective issuing authorities of currency. Thus, Feudal Money was synonymous with currency in circulation.

Money is a useful yardstick that measures relative contributions of owners in production besides that of OSM through a complex mechanism. Since OSM is subjugated to OMP by forced use of Pricing as the basis of negotiation in settling dues of labour, Money becomes common yardstick for both OSM and OMP, enabling comparison between OSM and OMP on same scale with Money.

P.21

With closer link between foreign trade and Capitalist production, leaning of Money, the richness indicator, on foreign trade is up. Relative inter-country foreign trade value-volumes to-and fro go long way in fixing rate of a Local Currency unit against Universal Currency.

Money is tripolar. One, liability discharge for production inputs by abstraction and carrying. Two, overreach to parallel space, e.g. agriculture, for ubiquity. Three, moderation by foreign trade.

1. Money is conceptually unique and the same in application in all countries worldwide. Richness is ability to generate Money yearly.

2. It relates to currency as $M = s_f * t_f * C_y$ [M=product in Money, C_y=product in currency, s_f=salability factor, t_f=foreign trade factor]

3. When the currency in consideration is the Universal Currency (U_c), value of t_f is taken as 1. That is, $M = s_f * U_c$. Thus, $U_c = t_f * C_y$.

4. t_f is a function of (a)foreign trade status that is, Current Ac balance (b)domestic production volume (c)surplus generation on satisfaction of domestic demand (d)exportability of domestic product (e)import control by substitution or cap.

5. Numeric value of t_f is country specific. Usually, t_f is a fraction less than 1. Higher the numeric value of t_f, stronger is the currency. Moreover, all t_f fractions in the world are inter-linked inversely. Thus, when t_f of one country rises it must cause t_f fractions to fall elsewhere.

Production causes influx of more Money into the system. The Central Bank is the main faucet through which Money is added to the system. Other Commercial Banks are conduits for such transfusion of Money using the modes of loan, rediscounting etc.

There is a note of discord imbedded in the fact that Money is essentially an offspring of the production module and conceptually it is alien to the agriculture module – its convenience notwithstanding. As such, in economies where agriculture has a dominant role to play dynamics of Money assumes a different character. In fact, as Money goes downstream, it finds seven different avenues and collect as distinct avatars in disparate Pools A (Agriculture), B_d (Builder), C_s (Consumer), D_b (Distributor), E_p (Entrepreneur), F_t (Foreign Trade) and G_v (Government).

As the economy expands, these exclusive Pools enlarge while maintaining inter-links. They are notionally put together to form a single entity called Money to give the economy semblance of unity, although it is only E_p that ploughs back directly into production mechanism.

Since avatar E_p is the one actually responsible for promotion of production and others are not, further expansion of Money would depend on what fraction of existing Money goes to E_p. Clearly, if E_p gradually loses its attractiveness as a destination of fresh Money as compared to other six destinations the economy would slow down as pace of an economy is proportional to fresh Money generation.

As such, economic policy prerogatives should be constituted around a two-pronged objective. One, to promote growth of fresh Money. Two, to help fresh Money head towards avatar E_p to the largest extent obviating the other avatars. Since a sizable bulk of fresh Money accumulates in avatar C_s before dissipating, failure to energize the movement from C_s to E_p could become a potent cause of economic decline. Similar reasons could be offered for movements between A and E_p.

Obstacles appearing in the way of implementation of such guidance are mostly of human origin such as taste, per-capita-income and income distribution. Disparity in income distribution is not only a social evil but it adversely affects propensity to purchase. If an amount of Money instead of being widely distributed is concentrated in a few hands, net purchase declines.

Increase in population encourages purchase that is, movement from C_s to E_p. However, rapid growth in population is not desirable as it can be associated with many unwelcome social problems. It is hardly prudent to invite multiple problems to solve one issue that is, economic growth. Moreover, if allowed a free run population has the tendency to accelerate and get out of control.

High growth rate of population is a double-edged sword – a boon and a bane simultaneously. Developed countries exploit the high population of underdeveloped countries for selling goods produced by them, keeping their own population growth under strict control.

Stimulation of production is possible through (a) Increase in Govt purchase that is, movement from avatar G_v to avatar E_p (b) Import substitution and export promotion that is, movement from F_t to E_p (c) Counselling people not to go for unproductive dead assets but buy goods that can be consumed that is, movement from B_d to E_p and (d) Impressing people not to lock funds in stock building that is, movement from D_b to E_p.

There is a tendency among agriculturists to maintain a distance from goods produced in factories. They are at war with producers and the bone of contention is Rate of Exchange (RoE). Inputs that Agriculture supplies to production undergoes hard bargaining. As such, rivalry and suspicion vitiates the relationship between the two sets of people.

Curiously, there is a fundamental difference in the perception of role of labour. Producers see labour as another input – faceless and nearly inanimate - but agriculturists see labour as a stake holder, albeit minor, in the output. The misgivings of agriculturists have to be addressed adequately for augmented A to E_p movement.

Since most economies of the world such as India's are not developed enough to be called Capitalist, the currency of such a country is tied to the Universal Currency which is nothing but the Currency of a developed Capitalist economy. This mechanism of bonding one minor Currency to another major, however developed, is a cause of inconsistency in the arrangement. Because, as the major suffers the minor is also hit for no fault of its own.

Thus, countries lacking a Capitalist machinery becomes a slave of another, developed Capitalist economy. The underdeveloped country receives undeserved reversals when fortunes of the Capitalist economy fluctuate for reasons to which the underdeveloped economy is entirely unrelated. For underdeveloped countries, F_t to E_p movement is difficult to achieve mainly because they are technologically backward and look to developed countries for their purchase of much needed sophisticated equipment and goods.

So, Money is like the homemaker in a large family of many heads who have divergent ideas and priorities. It has unlimited and often unreasonable demands placed on it but no one really cares for its health until it is grievously ill. The burden of expectations on it sometimes gets the better of Money.

Money imparts tangibility to economy which is regarded as intangible in many ways denying comparability and measurability without auxiliary assistance of Money. This role of Money makes it indispensable as tool in policy deliberations. Also, comparison among different economies becomes possible because of this role of Money.

Economic health has three ramifications namely, Pace (P_c), Quotience (Q_n) and Richness (R_n). Pace is a measure of the state of economic health in the short term, generally one year. Quotience is synergy profile of sectors in the economy and an index of lopsidedness. Most economies, except highly developed ones, are lopsided. Richness is pattern of economic growth in recent years.

If C_0 is taken as Currency generation in a particular accounting year and Money generation is M_0 then P_c is equivalent to M_0. Pace is more an indicator of current potential rather than prospects for the future.

In order to arrive at a pragmatic assessment of Quotience a few objective parameters need to be considered.

(a) Largeness of the economy or, the l factor which is ratio of size of the economy divided by size of the largest economy in the world.
(b) Evenness in spread of the economy that is, no over-dependence of the economy on production of a single item such as coffee.
(c) Human factors such as population, education and skill.
(d) Development status of industry, infrastructure and investment.
(e) Sufficiency of strength of agriculture to support the population.
(f) Social objectives such as healthcare, housing and employment.
(g) Stability of government and maturity of political system.

Richness or, pattern of growth should be unidirectional to be ideal. An economy that is used to having positive growth may go steadily up or may go up but slightly less steeply. If the growth is severely reduced it is a cause for concern. From pattern of growth future projection is possible that in many ways helps a prospective investor in his decision to invest.

Such forecast also helps in the policy making exercise. However, such forecasts are merely indicative and definitely not sacrosanct. Richness or, pattern of growth is a useful parameter within its limitations.

Economics is more concerned with fresh Money rather than stale Money. Vast oceans of stale Money possessed by a country does not ensure its economic dominance of world economic scenario unless it also tops in fresh Money generations, reflected as under.

$$D_d = (j_i * e_x + f_c)/(j_i * E_x + F).$$

The fraction D_d is Degree of Dominance, E_x is Existing (Stale) Money in world economy and F is Fresh (generation of) Money in world economy. The factors e_x and f_c are Existing and Fresh Money in the particular economy for the period under consideration and j_i is relative impact factor. Thus, while $(e_x + f_c)$ denotes Money content of an economy, $(j_i * e_x + f_c)$ gives its effective Money power.

Fresh Money in the hands of consumers that is, f_i, is qualitatively different from fresh Money in other pools. Consumption is the life of an economy, others are merely platforms supporting consumption.

The same quantum of fresh Money that enters a vast number of small pockets is much more potent than that enters a few big pockets. Spending by small pockets essentially relate to satisfaction of basic needs. Large number of unsatisfied basic needs is the normal order in poorer parts of the world. These wants add up to staggering levels only for the Capitalists to exploit these with willingness, vision and spirit while fulfilling their own economic agenda. Many exasperating issues of Capitalist system such as growth can be resolved - at least partially - if Capitalists take into cognizance the potentiality of People Power.

P.28

Everyone in this world, whose basic needs are satisfied, has a limit on willingness to spend and genuine interest in buying unless the buying options are mentally stirring enough. As such, an economy with a modest level of total personal income but with a high population has a greater potential than the economy with high personal total income level but low population.

UGLY MONEY, FAIR MONEY

Money : Menace of Toxicity in Over-Accumulation

As Money accumulates relentlessly, beyond a point, it inexorably leads to emergence of the phenomenon of Toxic Money - a spinoff from Capitalist process itself, arising from dearth of destinations for deployment of accumulated Money when it becomes huge.

```
                                          /--Production Purse(p_p)
                   /-- Vital Portfolio(V_t) --
                  /                       \-- Quenching Purse(q_p)
        Money(M) --
                  \                       /-- Retention Purse(r_p)
                   \-- Toxic Portfolio(T_x) --
                                          \--Speculation Purse(s_p)
```

$$F = g - (w + i + c + d) \quad [g\text{=goods sold, w=wages,}$$
$$i\text{=input,c=misc costs, d=distribution}]$$
$$F = E_{xI} - E_{x0} = (V_{tI} - V_{t0}) + (T_{xI} - T_{x0})$$
$$= (p_{pI} - p_{p0}) + (q_{pI} - q_{p0}) + (r_{pI} - r_{p0}) + (s_{pI} - s_{p0})$$

where F is Fresh Money influx and E_x is Existing Money in the system. In early stages of a Capitalist economy, growth needs and consumption needs are so acute that E_x almost entirely consists of Vital Money (V_t).

With passing time, Toxic Money (T_x) gradually surfaces.

At advanced stages, V_t and T_x are keen rivals for share of stale Money. Unfortunately, avenues of deployment of T_x are more numerous than that of V_t making growth of Money beyond a point a peril.

The Critical Index k represents degree of maturity of an economy.

$$k = 100 \cdot T_x / V_t \ \%.$$

T_x has the tendency to accumulate in a few pockets as opposed to many. People of questionable mindset, social orientation and commitment to human values often find themselves in possession of disproportionately huge funds seldom through honourable means.

Money grows inexorably quite like the Entropy of Thermodynamics. Fresh influx of Money in the system becomes a liability when k attains the critical mark of 25%. As all avenues of engaging Money in healthier areas through promotion of consumption are exhausted Speculation cannot be prevented. Backlash of such an eventuality depresses growth rate down to 1-2% despite strenuous attempts by policy makers to promote growth. It is a dilemma faced by all affluent developed economies derived from a malady intrinsic of Capitalism.

Unchained profusion of Money is an unbridled horse and a loose cannon which can have far greater nuisance value than their helpfulness. Growth, embodying the core of Capitalist motivation, cannot be sacrificed without getting rid of Capitalism altogether. Countries find themselves placed between deep sea and the devil.

One easy way-out would have been to seize Toxic Money and redistribute it among wage-earners in proportion of their respective wages. It cannot be acted upon as it goes contrary to the very theme of Capitalism. However, roundabout routes do exist.

Speculation is not supportive of the theme of Capitalism because it plays at best a passive role so far as promoting of growth is concerned. Speculation does not lead to creation of Money but makes Money redistributed in a way such that a few people become immensely rich at the expense of a large number of others. Speculation is jugglery but it allures people with examples of fairytale turn of fortune.

When Capitalism crosses the critical mark in its upward trajectory in an economy, it manifests a typical syndrome. It may be called the state of Super Capitalism. Here growth, inflation and population growth rates dwindle simultaneously as demands stand well satisfied. Recession becomes the rule rather than a periodic exception.

When an economy does not create much fresh Money, the prevailing interest rates are bound to be low. This could well be a likely cause of flight of Money to other economies where interest rates are higher. Weaker rival economies may gain strength as a consequence. As such, the think-tank cannot remain unconcerned with meagre growth rate.

To make matters worse, there is no fool-proof prescription to come out of such doldrums. It is an affliction much similar to slow-poisoning that does not kill immediately but slowly and surely pushes one towards death. Sooner or later a developed Capitalist economy has to enter the Super Capitalism phase where each country will have to sort out the problems with which it is beset. Lack of enough precedence may turn out to be a big disadvantage in speedy resolution of the complexities.

So, beleaguered large economies seek redemption through forced creation of an outlet of Money to foreign inferior economies in a two-pronged approach. This third category of Money serves as safety valve.

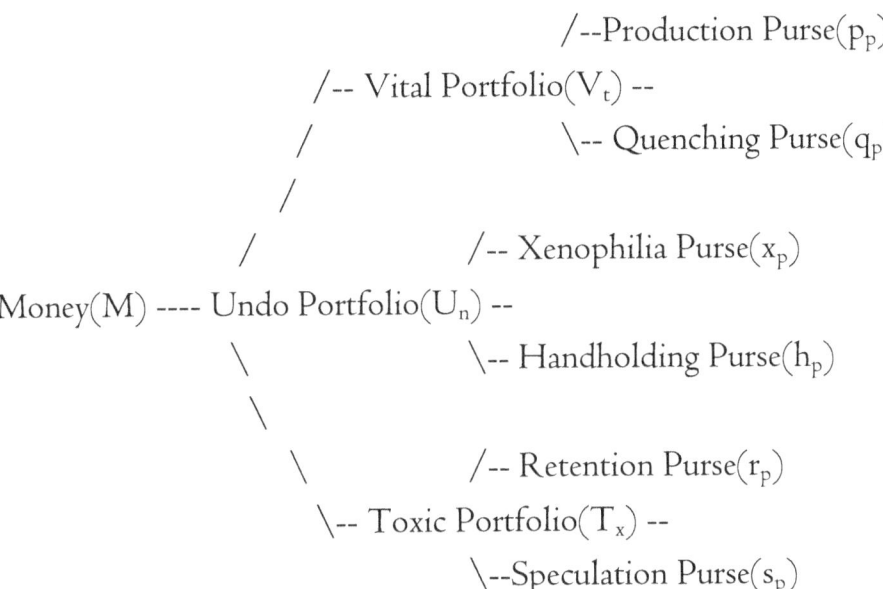

Thus the portfolio Undo Money (U_n) comes into existence in a desperate bid to undo the damage caused by Speculation Purse (s_p) and protect the large economy from potential disaster in the form of burgeoning s_p, by dissipation of T_x. U_n has two parts. Xenophilia (x_p) is dedicated to providing aid to weak economies to enable them to import more goods from the large economy. Handholding (h_p) is partial and selective transfer of technology to weak economies in joint collaborations having participation of giant corporations of the large economy but located in the underdeveloped country.

So, Money traversed a long way since early days of Capitalism when Industrial Revolution was still fresh at dawn of 19th century. Entire gamut of Money then consisted of Vital Portfolio (V_t). Demand for Money was very high for production (p_p) as well as for quenching (q_p) of needs that is, consumption. In time, Money creation accelerated.

The fifty-year period from 1935 to 1985 is conspicuous by a series of landmarks, forming economic attitudes across the world. After WWI came global recession culminating in Great Economic Depression of 1929-1935 when Money in hands of consumers declined alarmingly, demand nosedived and production dropped or halted, causing negative economic growth globally. Ever since, negative growth is a bugbear.

While countries like USA groped in the dark, Hitler's Germany and Swedes led by Gunnar Myrdal showed the light around 1933, with huge Govt spending, funded by unsecured borrowings, to give fillip to production and pep to economy[1]. Rest of Capitalist world emulated. It is a great irony of history that Keynes, who had apparently borrowed his theme from Hitler the loathed dictator, got lavish patronage of USA - for playing active role in pulling USA out of the rut - to be iconized as saviour[2] and propounder of an original theory in 1935. His rapid rise to fame reminds one of another British nobleman Duke of Wellington, hero of Waterloo at the expense of another autocrat, Napoleon — the latter vastly weakened in the aftermath of his terrible misadventure in invading Russia — who was already a broken man by then with his empire in tatters and his public life in its last throes.

1 J. K. Galbraith, "A History of Economics", p.222-25, 2 *ibid* p.225

We now present a rough outline of the series of crises that engulfed the world since 1929. The period 1929-35 marks the first phase of dialectical transformation or, Crisis-A - an aftermath of WWI. Attitudinal reaction in a concerted and universal manner with spontaneity and conviction is the cause that inexorably ushers in dialectical transformation. Thus, positive growth become a fixation with makers of economic policy since 1935.

Expansion of Money has its downturn in the form of lack of avenues of deployment. The second phase came around 1955-60 with Crisis-B in the wake of the Second Worls War (WWII), when Toxic Portfolio (T_x) grew into significance as the Critical Index k rose to become 10%. By that time, people had become more security conscious and more speculative. As the Mind-players made capital out of this emerging trend Speculation (s_p) established itself as a formidable rival to mainstream economy and a growing irritant to policy makers. Policy makers, though, did not have a clue how to handle the situation and left the problem poorly addressed using wrong prescriptions until s_p became menacingly high.

Their reaction was passive, muted and limited to formation of the world bodies The World Bank (WB) and the International Monetary Fund (IMF) in the wake of WWII. Both WB and IMF started as rebuilding funds to address the devastation of WWII but in due course morphed into diversion windows for excess Money before it turned Toxic. Large economies formed lender-groups replacing individual economies. These economies were stirred into decisive action when opportunity to rebuild came following WWII.

Continued lack of tactical understanding on the part of policy makers worsened the situation. As crisis snowballed drastic action was required. The think-tank desperately looked for reprieve. The synthetic Undo Portfolio (U_n) was created with a widened scope to siphon off excess Money to weak economies before it went to Toxic Portfolio (T_x). It was a gambit because it nurtured potential rivals.

It was also a dialectical necessity that brought big economies on road to equity. In a parallel move foreign trade reform was conducted by calling the Bretton-Woods (BW) conference in 1971 to start with to rework the monetary arrangement existing internationally. It marks the third phase of dialectical change as k rose to 25% to throw the system into chaos and invited Crisis-C.

Crisis-D was precipitated in 1991 with emergence of China as the fastest growing economy in the world followed by India. The risk taken by the developed countries in opening the Undo Portfolio backfired as small economies grew in strength to be reckoned as important players. Value of k could not be brought down or even arrested at a reasonable level as it climbed to 30% and remained a cause for perpetual worry. China saved USA from the disgrace of losing value of its currency as China purchased huge amounts of USA Govt bonds denominated in Dollars so that its own currency remained low in value vis-à-vis the Dollar to help boost its exports. China had the blueprint of progress ready before it had embarked on its all-out drive to ensure employment for the masses as it targeted not only its vast domestic market but also the global market with its most potent weapon, the crux of Crisis-D, RoE.

The World Wars might not have been direct causes of change in the character of Money but certainly were shakers of the human mind that brought a measure of desperation in thinking necessary for knee-jerk reaction. As Capitalism developed, mostly meeting ordinary needs, it acted as deterrent to growth in production and stagnation set in.

Stagnation led to the reincarnation of RoE as a powerful game changer in post-WWII scenario. To cope with falling demands due to saturation of ordinary needs production required an impetus. Obvious recourse was forced rise in the RoE of need items. While it raised the production value it left the buyers short on buying power and looking for more income. Incomes were raised too but with a time lag just long enough to allow economy to register growth higher than income raise. More Money with consumers encouraged further rise in RoEs resulting in a vicious circle that put RoE of ordinary items in a spiral.

In developing countries such as China RoE remained firm. With vast production capacity for ordinary products and cheaper RoE they dominated international market. Emergence of China as a key player in foreign trade indicates yet another dialectical shift.

It is likely that China will catch up with major Capitalist countries and come to display the same syndrome with which present day Capitalists are afflicted. As the malady is intrinsic in Capitalism, it can hardly be addressed adequately or even mitigated to exercise control over it. Probably morbid fear of negative growth prevents the think-tank to shrug off Keynesian dogma and face modern day problems of the world with a modern mindset.

Money, around which the present global economic order works, having been erected as a denatured storage of work done only by MoP over endless ongoing cycles, is an imposition, a denial — both through application of brute force in a skewed system - and a recognition of the supremacy of MoP over Humanity in Toil (HiT) — the latter being a combination of Manpower on one hand and Innovation, Skill and Scholarship on the other.

While the fact of absolute, unmitigated and complete ownership of MoP over the entire reward for efforts taken jointly by MoP and HiT invites indignation, for even the meagre compensation that HiT gets for being a factor in Production and Production-plus it has to indulge in endless strife. This system entitles one partner to receive the reward at the expense of the other who is left to fend for itself and fight for small compensations. Transparency and fairness, if any, existing in the extant process of evaluation of relative contributions to creation of Production and Production-plus are hard to see.

```
                              |--- MoP 100% ---→ Money accrues &
        Reward for ----------|                   adds to existing Money
        Production work       |--- HiT 0%

                              |--- MoP ----→ Major share
        Money accrual ------ | --- HiT ---→ Minor share by Bargain
                              | --- Inputs ---→ Minor share by Market
                                                      (of Production)
```

P.39

Thus, Money has two facets. It is a useful scale for comparison of relative contributions to Production work among MoPs, a form of recompense for Production work by HiT. Money-with-Hit induces Money into circulation with birth of Market. For a healthy Market, enlargement of Money-with-Hit must keep pace with expansion of Capacity else Circulation becomes static.

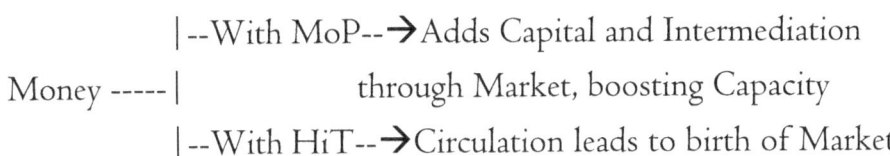

```
                                        /--Fuels Production
                      |--Consumption--
                      |     (major)     \-- Fuels Business
                      |
Money-with-HiT --- |--Savings--→ Transforms to Investment
Functioning as the |              (minor)/Capital(direct), Capacity
Prime Mover of     |
Market mechanism   |--Savings--→ Transforms to Investment
                                 |(minor)/Capital (through inter-
                                 |-mediary), Capacity
```

Capital comes from Investment. It gets boosted when Savings increases. If Savings needs to go up, Consumption must go down.

P.40

Market, net of Money (M) movements in a honeycomb grid, has four chambers H-C-B-A, i.e., M=A+B+C+H, five windows with Net Rates of Flow n_1-n_2-n_3-n_4-n_5 and nine interfaces f_1.H-C, f_2.H-B (2-way), f_3.H-A (2-way), f_4.C-B (2-way), f_5.B-A (2-way).

```
|------------------------------------------------------------|
|                                                            |
|                        2HiT (H)                            |
|--------f₁(n₁)--------|--------f₂(n₂)--------|--------f₃(n₃)------|
|     1Capa (C)    f₄(n₄)  3Busi (B)   f₅(n₅)    4Agri(A)    |
|----------------------|----------------------|--------------|
```

Agriculture (A) has its own Production system but it is not independent of the Market. The need to have producer and seller roles segregated sees Business (B) evolve as a mediator for unified logistics and RoE matrix.

Each Interface creates an exclusive Pocket-in-Market (PiM) or, p_i. As Money is in Dynamic Equilibrium, at a randomly picked point of time relative concentrations of Money in the four PiMs q_1-q_2-q_3-q_4 depend on the Relative Net Rates of Flow r_1-r_2-r_3-r_4 that is, q_i varies as r_i, $r_1=n_4-n_1$, $r_2=n_1-n_2-n_3$, $r_3=n_2-n_4-n_5$, $r_4=n_5-n_3$.

```
|------------------------------------------------------------|
|                                                            |
|                        p₂ (q₂,r₂)                          |
|----------------------|------------------------|------------|
|    p₁ (q₁,r₁)    |    p₃ (q₃,r₃)     |    p₄ (q₄,r₄)       |
|------------------|--------------------|--------------------|
```

As cycles go on, more work is done by MoP creating more Money and adding on to the vastness of Money. Not all of this incremental Money finds its way to augmentation of C though. Parts of it, by cunning ploy of contra-interests, are deliberately trapped in pipelines, niches, nooks and corners for eventual diversion to B and A.

Money cannot be saved or locked up in a chest. Money is characterized by its continuous flow. Only the flow can be slowed down by counter-flow from the opposite direction, as it happens in the case of H--→B and B--→C movements – in the first case counter-flow is caused by payment of wages by B to H and in the second it is due to purchase of raw materials by C from B. As such, Money at H and B pockets fail to rotate in good time in order to reach pocket C before end of current cycle and accumulate.

Two-way movement is also witnessed between pockets H and A as well as between B and A, the first relating to payment of wages and the second to purchase of agricultural commodities on one hand and sale of agricultural inputs on the other.

G_r'%, Money actually travelling timely to join Capital by recycle, is the Effective Indicator of Growth (EIG). Since Money gets created in repetitive cycles, it is a question of how fast Money travels to its destination i.e., Capital, before commencement of the next cycle rather than how much of it travels on a timeless journey.

Money is unilateral and indestructible too. It has endless growth. Neither consumption can quench it nor stock market can inflate it. It takes its own course through time. Mobile Money adds on to C (Capacity, Core, domain MoP). On losing motion, it gathers as B_s (Bogus Capital, Buffer, domain Business), A (Aloof Capital, Appendage, domain Agriculture) and H (No Capital, domain HiT). A, B, H cannot reproduce Money.

If Money grows at G_r% per cycle, then C grows at a depleted rate $G_r' = G_r \cdot (1 - X_l)$, where X_l is Lapse-out, a fraction that fails to plough back to C timely and adds to B and A instead. As $\char94 B >> \char94 A$, we get,

$$X_l = O_b \cdot I_b / (P_r \cdot D_w) = \char94 B / (\char94 B + \char94 C) = Y_f / (1 + Y_f)$$

where $Y_f = \char94 B / \char94 C$, $\char94$ is differential or growth, O_b is Obstruction, I_b is Inhibition, P_r is Pressure and D_w is Door-width, all fractions of the ideal. While O_b is caused by cross-currents in B_u, I_b is linked to ethos, ignorance, health etc. P_r relates to marketing and D_w is based on living standard. We have,

$$1/X_l = P_r \cdot D_w / (O_b \cdot I_b) = 1 + (\char94 C / \char94 B) = 1 + (1/Y_f)$$
$$\text{or, } \char94 C / \char94 B = (1/X_l) - 1 = 1/Y_f = (P_r \cdot D_w / (O_b \cdot I_b)) - 1.$$

$\char94 A$ is also affected by a factor Divergence of Perception (DoP). For a new product its Worth for the seller may not match its Utility to the buyer. Worth and Utility rarely match, particularly for new products. Slow acceptance makes aberration from DoP inevitable.

P.43

Let ^V% be growth in Volume of production during a cycle, as measured from seller's point of view based on production data. Let N_o=Worth/Utility be normalization factor for DoP and E_f an emergent factor. Then,

$$\wedge V = G_r'.N_o.(1-E_f) = G_r.(1-X_1).N_o.(1-E_f)$$

or, $\wedge V = G_r.N_o.(1-E_f)/(1+Y_f) = j_c/(1+Y_f)$

or, $\wedge V = j_c/(1+1/((P_r.D_w/O_b.I_b)-1))$.

Where j_c is constant in the short-term. In advanced economy, as cycles go on, products get more and more versatile and sophisticated and N_o rises in the product-mix i.e., N_{o2}/N_{o1} is >1. Under growing severity of competition E_f enlarges, so, $(1-E_{f2})/(1-E_{f1})$ is <1. As G_{r2}/G_{r1} hovers around +1, for fixing the peg ^V relies on O_b, P_r, I_b, N_o, E_f and D_w else, on Y_f in short-term.

In a lagging economy, as products are traditional, N_o is close to 1. ^V has O_b, P_r, I_b, E_f and D_o else, Y_f in short-term as fixers of peg.

Character of G_r' is in sync with the objective of Economics which is to find the means whereby the concentration of Money at C maximizes, thus making concentrations in rest of the Honeycomb namely, at B, A and H irrelevant and counter-productive. Money, because of this characteristics imposed on it, comes to resemble Entropy of Thermodynamics.

P.44

Burgeoning B is the bugbear that an economy has to face. While B is incapable of reproducing Money, it generates Services (S), making Money change hands with resultant complexity and Obstruction (O_b) to Money on its way to joining C and thus to becoming C-money. So, using B-money, B runs S - an Economy-within-Economy (EwE) - choking growth of C. S, an offshoot of B, has its own plans of growth ($^\wedge$S) that act contrary to growth of the economy. Similarly, A has its own variety of Money (A-money) and own design of growth ($^\wedge$A) - it has a demarcated area though.

The functional role that Money occupies in the Capitalist System has so many ramifications that any direct modification attempt on Money may face inhibition for the uncontrollable repercussions it may generate. Since our ultimate aim is to put Money on a higher pedestal that gives a uniform view of the entire populace, we shall presently look for Facilitators of Change that would put Money in right track for that pedestal. It is interesting to note that seeds of change lie imbedded and dormant in age-old concepts, only they need rediscovery and enlivenment through modification and adaptation to a new perspective.

UGLY MONEY, FAIR MONEY

C*HAPTER* ~ 5 ~

Mobility Profile of Money : Trans-cycle Accumulation by Growth, Savings, Interest, Intermediation and Investment

Our first step in reaching out to Facilitators of Change brings us in close contact with phenomena that give Money a Mobility Profile. Of these, Growth is accumulation of Money across cycles, Interest is its outcrop.

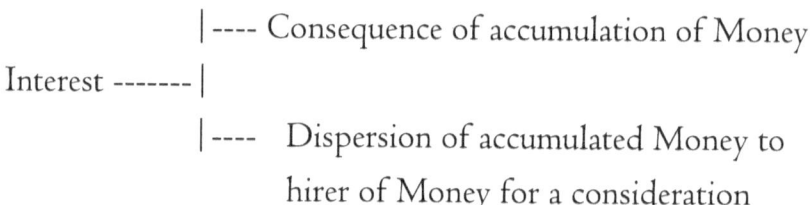

It is axiomatic that Money would grow as cycles move on. Business (B), the principal receptacle as well as moiety of inert Money accumulates inert Money left behind by previous cycles. It acts as buffer making current Money available to Capacity (C) on credit as also in siphoning capital Money to C on loan to make up for any inadequacy of Growth of Capacity (^C) that often upsets growth plans.

Thus, time-lag in realization of ^C can be neutralized and paucity of ^C can boosted and the entire shortage met by B through siphoning, called Finance, with the condition that B is to be compensated with the share of growth achieved by C at the rate of I_r part. I_r is the rate of Interest, expressed in %. Siphoning occurs by Intermediation of Banks. So, B is the Bridge for or key to inter-cycle communication.

A, the other moiety of inert Money, has a withdrawn existence. B tries to involve A in the role of indirect aid to production through financial initiatives such as contract farming, commercial farming and large scale cultivation by mechanical aid and upgraded input.

Over cycles, as M becomes larger, B has an ever increasing control-by-proxy role to play as to policy and planning the growth of C.

Growth of Money is an integral conceptual part of the Capitalist order. Money, an imaginary repository for productive efforts of people, is combined and pooled through time and across cycles. Since people work ceaselessly, Money goes on growing endlessly.

Let us conceive of an imaginary situation where all products produced simultaneously in production cycles, of equal length for all products, come one after another in distinct space of time. At the juncture where one production cycle comes to a close and the next is about to begin, those intending to undertake a journey through production path look for resources for the journey in the form of Money.

Money-bags, unproductive though they are, come forward to lend Money but for a compensation to be carved out of gains emerging from next cycle's productive efforts. Money-bags do nothing to earn such a portion of productive efforts of other people. This effortless, idle and base appropriation of Money is called Interest - a reward for doing nothing except owning Money.

Interest is the crucial feature that generates mobility in Money. Without Interest Money would lie in inertia in the hands of unproductive people while productive people will remain grounded for want of Money without which productive efforts do not take off at all. Since for this *modus operandi* Money-support is fundamental, Interest becomes key to sustainability of Capitalism.

Interest is redistribution of earners' rewards among non-earners under compulsion mainly through agency of the Bank – a process known as Intermediation. Although degenerative as an idle earning, its merits lie in bringing reprieve to the infirm, old etc.

So, Money, unless it has the associated benefit of Interest, is useless in the hands of unproductive people except for spending on consumption. Interest induces Savings by reducing consumption.

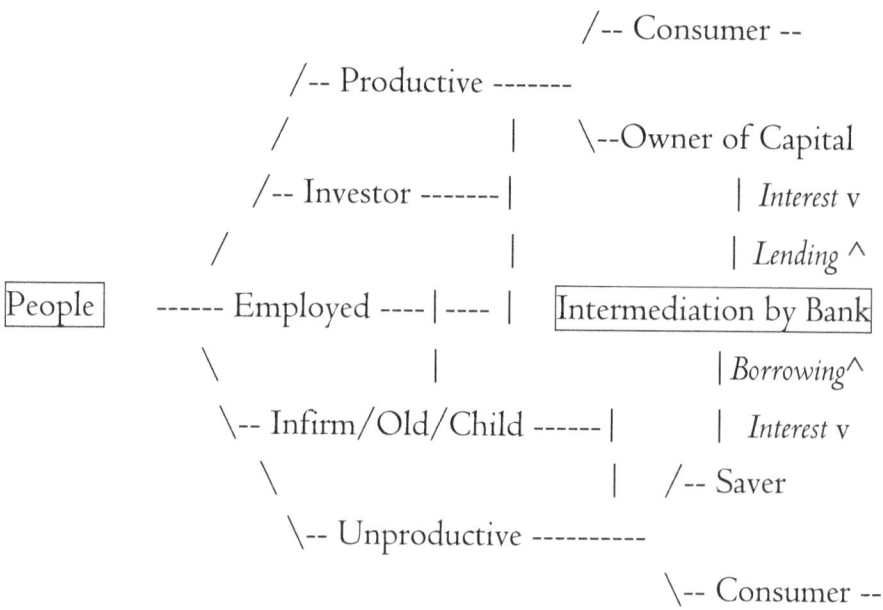

It is rare to find People engaged in roles other than multifaceted roles vis-a-vis Money. Thus, an employee at a workplace is a saver with a Bank, an investor in stock market besides being a consumer. As such, segregating people along the lines of demarcation as above is not feasible.

Savings binds Intermediation and Investment in a circular relationship breached by production cycle-ends. People may directly use Money as Owner's Capital or, indirectly come into Ownership of Capital through Investment in primary or secondary stock market (SSM). Entire Capitalist structure gyrates on Savings inspired by Interest. But, as Capitalism spreads its wings, production multiplies and need to arouse consumption gets direr. Low Interest rates divert focus from Savings to consumption.

Secondary stock market is the place where stocks are resold at a higher price with the aim of making gain. Such transactions merely make Money change hand without extending any support to the process of production. It has close resemblance to gambling.

This retrograde aspect of Capitalist system assumes key system role since, when share index rises marking upward revaluation of trading prices of key shares, static Money enters share market from other sectors of economy. Sellers get liquidity and buying power in hand to turns market lively. Thus, static Money morphs into mobile Money. So, effect of trading in secondary share is to impart enhanced mobility to Money and enliven market.

It appears that, SSM, although just an auxiliary to the main structure on which the Capitalist economy performs, has a larger role to play especially in the context of economic depression in mature economies. Foreign Money in SSM is an even bigger help.

P.50

The Bank, playing central mobilizer role in Capitalist system as principal Lender, make its gains from the difference in Interest it gets from the Producer and Interest it pays to Savings. Bank's intermediation ensures production and succour to the infirm. Savings rides the workhorse called Money to make it mobile but cannot give an insight into Money.

Again, another negative aspect of the system becomes a prime mover of the system because Money begets Money through production and it costs to get Money needed for production.

Interest rate is not Bank's prime concern but difference between earning rate of Interest on fund lent to producer and paying rate of Interest on fund deposited by saver is. Funds offered to producers at very low interest rates stimulate productive activity. This practice is adopted by developed economies around the world by setting Central Bank's benchmark Interest rate very low. USA, the largest Capitalist economy, which has the world's authorization to print unlimited currency, even goes to the extent of providing Money at zero rate of Interest to producers of goods.

Accepting not so honourable facets of life as part and parcel of the way life exists and incorporating their dubious values into the value systems has its flip side too. In a simile, one has to keep in mind what the bovines had been fed with when a Mad-ox like syndrome erupts, as the syndrome could get beyond redress otherwise.

The Mobility Profile is proficient in tracking down outward performance of Money. It is unaware of the inward inadequacies that Money may have been carrying because Mobility Profile knows Money only from its Usage. It is quite in the dark as to the inner constituency of Money. As such, when grievous afflictions grip the economy with its origin lying inside the corpus of Money, Mobility Profile flounders. That makes exploration of other options that give access to the internal structure of Money a necessity.

Money has two functional aspects. One is Pricing and the other is Mobility Profile. Doing away with Mobility Profile invites total collapse of the Capitalist structure. Even, modifications of large dimensions in it are likely to throw the system in disarray and the resulting tangle could be so utterly unresolvable that it may end up in breakdown. As such, Mobility Profile being delicately poised and intricately structured, it is eminently sane to leave Mobility Profile untouched. Keeping it intact, we can turn our attention to Pricing.

This is the critical point that defines the line of thinking that is central to this writing. We have to keep revolutionary aspirations, if any, in the back-burner while we stretch our imaginations by adopting an approach that is neither too far from the reality so as to be utopian nor so drastic that it cannot be reconciled with the existing reality - making convergence with reality possible through intelligent and thoughtful application of available options. Throwing the system in complete disarray is not desirable as millions could be affected by such action and since it is the people whose interests is central objective of our efforts.

P.52

New ideas to replace the old and the entrenched ones do not come easily and automatically. We have tried out our experimentation in a specific direction, hoping for good and compelling results.

While residing inside the house offered by conventional wisdom we do not stop ourselves from inviting our guests – the radical ideas. Whether the guests stay there for the time being or for all time from here onwards is a decision we cannot take.

UGLY MONEY, FAIR MONEY

CHAPTER ~ 6 ~

Beacons of Pricing-Evolution : Quiddity, Monery and Normey

P.54

We have reached a stage where, to advance further, we need to look up to Beacons of Pricing-evolution for leads, in a radical vein, junking the static classical mould in which facilitators of change have no place. It is the limiting point beyond which classical mould fails.

Till the State steps in to protect interests of helpless people we have to maintain Mobility Profile as it is but that does not stop us from ameliorating Pricing and making it inclusive, starting with intrinsic value of saleables. Dearth of materials is a stumbling block in defining Money.

We take an indirect route through retro-definitions and institute a demi-form of Money from its present state of formlessness, hoping to reach a definition of Money finally.

Money at micro level needs a relook. Fresh Money (F) spawns as :

$$F = g - (w + i + c + d)$$

[g = goods sold, w=wages, i=input, c=misc costs, d=distribution].

Variable g has wider and deeper ramifications than is apparent. Economy advances with growth which depends on generation of Fresh Money (F) which is goods sold less wages, input and other costs. However, the sale proceeds of goods is dependent on both the Rate of exchange, RoE (R), it fetches and the Volume (V) of sale.

$$F = (R \cdot V) - (w + i + c + d)$$

RoE is highly subjective. It is purchaser's volition or, stamp of his willingness given in notional auction. Intrinsic Product quality is a distant cousin to RoE – related, but too feebly to be called a relative.

Being forced to depend on fickle and volatile human mind for cognition, Money has to cede on consistency, key eligibility aspect of building material for Paradigm. Money has blinkered vision too of role of Inputs namely, Agriculture & Mining (A&M) and Labour & Mindwork (L&M) or just A and L. Unless the roles of A and L in Money are put in right perspective, weak economies of the world escape understanding.

Taking G for Goods produced we bring into reckoning an alternative extended version of Money or, Monery (M') with the following features in which O stands for Outgo and subscripts g, a, l stand for goods, agriculture and labour. As Money (M) derives its retro-definition from fresh accumulation of Money (F), fresh accumulation of Monery (F') retro-defines Monery (M').

$$F' = [(R_g \cdot V_g) + (R_a \cdot V_a) + (R_l \cdot V_l)] - (O_g + O_a + O_l)$$
$$O = w + i + c + d$$
$$F' - F = [(R_a \cdot V_a) + (R_l \cdot V_l)] - (O_a + O_l)$$
$$q = (F' - F)/F = (F'/F) - 1.$$

This approach recognizes Agriculture and Labour as having their own outputs which are very high in Underdeveloped Economies (UE) and, as such, not inconsequential at all. RoE for such outputs namely, crop and toil vis-à-vis produced goods is critical factor in emplacing an UE.

If value of production of goods is far greater than that of Agriculture and Labour, as in developed economies, then F' approaches F and M' approaches M as divergence q nears zero.

Money has no definition. The route to its definition in absolute terms - detached from its Usage - being tortuous and uncertain as well as space, time and effort consuming, we settle for the second best - retro-definition. It draws on F, which is Usage-related, and links F to M through inductive reasoning, with exact relationship and accurate mathematical nexus unspecified.

As retro-definition eludes the roots and is shorn of aura of fundamentality, it is short of a proper definition but is arguably superior to mere perception for being amenable to mathematical treatment.

Retro-definition does not give true access to Money but measuring Money in its entirety and appraising it in its absolute form is of no real use, only inflow of Fresh Money (F) matters for all practical purposes. So, retro-definition is adequate for use in Paradigm.

The stage is now set for first of two breakaway leaps. Here we create F', a parallel of F, that has widened scope, with further intention of synthesizing from F', M', a parallel of M, retaining the reverse algorithm that exists between F and M. That is, we extend the reverse algorithm to Monery, M', replace F with F' and mark shift in values of g, a and l. As such, concept of growth as inflow of Fresh Monery, F', replaces that of Fresh Money, F.

The door now partly opens for entry of inclusiveness. Monery, first among the beacons of Pricing-evolution, stands familiarized and we have now succeeded in letting people hear the sound of revving up of the engine of change. Inclusiveness is a close associate of equitability. We are now equipped with an instrument that pinpoints the source of cheating and measures its extent. The truism that knowledge is the greatest source of strength and that it unites people on a common purpose can be a motivation in installing Monery as a policy guide and basis of Pricing by stripping Money of this role while letting Money to continue as medium of exchange.

Let us compare negative growth situations. Downward spiral in all economic parameters associated with negative growth in Money that is, -F, in immature economies (IE) with low k is intractable even if it is a large economy (LE) with small q. If the LE is highly mature and T_x is large such fear is really unfounded. Negative growth in Monery that is, -F', could wreak as much havoc as F. Albeit, –F' occurring in UE is a distant possibility for some reasons.

In UE, where q is large, a and l are dominant components of F' with g taking a backseat. M' in the hands of consumers too will diminish like M does if industry suffers and G has a temporary freefall but here the downward spiral gets arrested at a level with support from A and L. In UE, agricultural income of suppliers of input, food and labour is crucial as source of consumption. G, A and L are co-actors in shaping the economy as against G only in case of LE.

Economic policy makers in UE should get rid of the fixation that deadly fear of negative growth brings. They should instead orient their thoughts towards sustaining growth in employment, per capita income and equitability in income distribution to get social priorities right. Once the fixation is off their minds they can embark on policies that combine the apparently discordant principles of Welfare State and Capitalist State seamlessly, squeezing Toxic Money in the process. UE policy making must be pragmatic in not replicating Western economic doctrine. China again leads the way.

```
                                        /--Production Purse(p_p)
                    |--- Vital Portfolio(V_t) ---
                    |                   \-- Quenching Purse(q_p)
                    |
                    |                   /-- Xenophilia Purse(x_p)
                    |--- Undo Portfolio(U_n) ---
                    |                   \--Handholder Purse(h_p)
    Money(M) ---
                    |                   /-- Retention Purse(r_p)
                    |--- Toxic Portfolio(T_x) ---
                    |                   \--Speculation Purse(s_p)
                    |
                    |                   /-- Exigency Purse(e_p)
                    |--- Welfare Portfolio (W_f) ---
                                        \--Fortification Purse(f_p)
```

W_f, in pre-WWII at early immature stages of development of Capitalism, was regarded as symptomatic of Socialism when k was low and T_x was also low or non-existent. Generation of fresh Money could hardly meet the burgeoning demands of production and consumption. Then, with attaining of maturity of Capitalism and surfeit of Money, W_f became just an option within the Capitalist framework. Still, W_f remained as untouchable as in the early days of Capitalism and abhorrence towards W_f, that grew out of stale textual contents, was more of a cultivation to keep alive in public psyche a dogmatic distance from Socialism than it was a tactical necessity. In this milieu of obduracy, China grabbed the initiative.

A major area for free play of T_x is the Secondary Share Market (SSM). SSM activity is akin to gambling. SSM operations are essentially hand-changing exercise of Money among opportunists devoid of any positive economic implications. They contribute nothing to economic growth except that when there is a share market boom, small shareholders tend to redeem their holdings and that adds to consumption increasing the already unseemly distortion in money distribution in the process. That is, a small part of the Money usurped by the share market moves from T_x to V_t.

While Primary Share Market (PSM) is largely attuned to investment, SSM is entirely speculation oriented. Regrettably, people like Warren Buffet who make fabulous Money through SSM using Toxic Money are deified. Undue pride in Capitalist tradition deprives many rich countries to come out of this rut.

If Money is to assume the status of embodiment of efforts of both man and machine it cannot disregard contributions of the inputs A and L going into production of goods. Monery is more inclusive and more comprehensive in this regard. However, the mechanism of fixing RoE of A, L and G that leave them exposed to vagaries of the market is a common weakness of both M and M'.

The difference between M' and M essentially lies in the fact that M' is composite while M is unipolar. M' has multiple areas of output and income associated with it in the form of crops and minerals in A, mandays in L and production of goods and services in G while M is limited to production of goods and services in G only. Inputs are not considered as Money spinners.

Secondly, consumption is buffered in M' as besides being input to G A generates other crops the most vital of which all, food, is universally consumed unabated irrespective of production of goods. A also creates its own income. Basic food consumption is unrelated to income except in famine. L also has its own work output and income generation.

Thirdly, G is endowed with one exclusive feature, Capacity (C) which in association with Technology (T) is a formidable productive power and resource, making LE economically superior. LE cannot afford to allow circumstances that render C and T_c idle because both C and T_c go into obsolescence fast. So, keeping C and T_c mobile is a cardinal aspect of production of goods and services but of lesser relevance to agriculture and mining. So, M has its priority well defined but M' has multiple priorities spread over A, L and G that need balancing.

P.61

Let us get back to the basic equations that define inflow of fresh Money and fresh Monery.

$$F = (R_g \cdot V_g) - O_g$$
$$F' = [(R_g \cdot V_g) + (R_a \cdot V_a) + (R_1 \cdot V_1)] - (O_g + O_a + O_1).$$

As dictated by the market, not only do the RoEs R_g, R_a and R_1 vary but relative values R_g/R_a, R_a/R_1 and R_1/R_g are also changeable. So are V_g, V_a and V_1 and O_g, O_a and O_1. As Pricing does not truthfully interpret human and mechanical efforts in creating product, crop or mandays invocation of concept of Consumer Indifference as embodied in I, Insipidity Coefficient, to link Money to true efforts of man and machine, becomes necessary.

Let us get Intrinsic Value of an item, its Quiddity (Q), as also the second facilitator of change, to replace RoE. Q is related directly to efforts of man and machine rather than to consumer's choice as in case of RoE. Arguably, lack of appeal makes a product insipid.

$$R = Q \cdot I$$

where Q is constant while R and I variables.

I, Insipidity Coefficient, lives in the consumer's mind. Usually, R is less than Q and I is a fraction less than I with upper limit of I. Aberrations make R > Q and I > I occurring mostly with craze and luxury items like objects of art.

I, of mental origin, is a complex of three curbing factors 1.Social sanction (S_s) 2.Trendability (T_r) 3.Usurption (U_s). While S_s and U_s are fractions less than 1, T_r ranges from zero to numbers far greater than 1. RoE is not fixed by individual discernment but by collective receptivity of the majority.

As such, trendy items for which a space has already been created in receptive minds, mostly young, through ads has a high I value. Agro commodities, unexciting as they are, get only low I values. Items that help flaunt social status are in high demand. Thus, possession of a car – whether that fulfills a necessity or not – becomes a priority and purchased, even if it is unaffordable, in instalment payment.

Growers of perishable agro crops – most of whom in India are poor farmers with no facility for preservation - are subjected to rampant exploitation and get a low I value from the consumers. They are not united enough in rate negotiations with middlemen, cold storages and shopping malls who are the bulk purchasers. To add to the woes of the farmers, vested interests, who play a part in pushing value of I lower down for cut money, are generally holders of political power too.

Shopping malls, by adding flavours of glitz and glamour of appearance to preservation capacity and home delivery, capture the space between the consumer and the farmer. They get a much higher I value from consumers as compared to farmers. The same applies to commercial crops such as jute which, although not perishable, fail to get the right I value from purchasers who are not individuals but are owners of mills. They are far more united than individuals in exploiting growers.

Where usurption rules, I has miserably low and nakedly skewed profile, needing Govt support.

The gradient of a plot of R against I would give Q. So, a better elementary understanding of I could open up vast possibilities. I is related to its components in the following manner.

$$I = X \cdot Y_s \cdot Y_u / Z$$

Where X is Eccentricity of market related to volatility and variable with market conditions such as supply, seasonality, contingencies etc. It is a fraction with maximum possible value of 1.

Each individual component now needs quantification. While both Y_s and Y_u are social ills subject to slow transformation, Z_t, aligned to modern age technology and ad, changes fast. In the short term,

$$I = X \cdot Y \cdot Z_t / (Z_t - 1)$$

Obstructivity, $Y = (Y_s \cdot Y_u)$, is constant in short term with both Y_s and Y_u about 0.8 for India and $Y = 0.64$, subject to optimization. To make it easy we put $Z = 1 - (1 / Z_t)$ where Z_t, Trend-sensitivity, is a numeral and a product of six sub-Zs with values between 1-10.

Trend-sensitivity is a quality that varies widely among items but for any one item movement space is narrow. Rationally devised relative numeric values have to be assigned to sub-Zs in the range 1–10. For offbeat items like objects of art sub-Z can be negative.

P.64

The sub-Zs are (a) Universality (Z_u) or mass appeal (b) Purpose (Z_p) or importance of use, (c) Gradation (Z_g) or scale of choice, (d) Sophistication or speciality of applications (Z_s), (e) Criticality (Z_c) or acuteness of need which is 10 for a life-saving drug and (f) Discernment (Z_d) or educated selection based on technical features.

Example of an item belonging to Universality - Consumer Electronics, Purpose - Communications with Sophistication, Criticality and Discernment as none is mobile handset. For a top class mobile handset Z_t is product of Z_u(Consumer Electronics), Z_p(Communications) and Z_g(High-end) - all numerals in the scale 1-10.

All sub-Z cannot be 1 at a time. Z_u is 10 for products of high market focus used by a wide cross-section of people while Z_p is 10 for life-style defining products. Z_s is 10 for products of superior technology and extraordinary use like aeroplanes.

For the top class mobile handset Z_u, Z_p and Z_g are nearly 10 while Z_s, Z_c and Z_d have default value of 1, being inapplicable, making Z_t close to 1000 and Z converge to 1.

```
                          /----- Zu -- universality
             /-----General Sub-Zs ------ Zp -- purpose
            /             \----- Zg -- gradation
   Zt ------
            \             /----- Zs -- sophistication
             \-----Special Sub-Zs ------ Zc -- criticality
                          \----- Zd -- discernment
```

P.65

The value of Z thus obtained is only relative but that does not prevent us from getting at the true estimate of Q using the equation

$$R = Q . I$$
$$\text{or, } R = Q . X . Y / Z$$
$$\text{or, } R . X_m = (Q . Y / Z) . (X_d + X_s) . X_m / 100$$
$$\text{or, } R = (Q . Y / Z) . (X_d + X_s) / 100$$

In this general relationship equation X_d is drift in the short term, X_s is long term shift due to qualitative changes and X_m is monetary impact of currency revaluation which is ignorable as it affects R and Q equally. In the short term, for a specific product and domain Z, Q and Y are constant. If market conditions are perfect, X_s is 0. Taking the first steady market situation soon after 01.01.2000 as base at which point $X_d = 0$ and $X_s = 100$, we get,

$$R_{00} = Q . (X_{d00} + X_{s00}) . Y / Z$$
$$\text{or, } R_{00} = Q . (0 + 100) . Y / (100 . T) = Q . Y / Z.$$

Since Z and Y are known, we get the value of Q from R_{00}. For all market situations,

$$R = R_{00} . (X_d + X_s) / 100 = R_{00} . X_s / 100 \quad [\text{ as } X_s >> X_d].$$

Using this general relationship X_s can be found out from R as R_{00} is known.

I is rendered inelastic with intention since drastic change in it might tumble the existing economic order dramatically. In UE like India there is wide scope for management of I.

We have discussed how shopping malls stepped in into the lucrative space between growers of agricultural commodities and the consumer. Another area is the fascination that works in consumers' minds in India that tends to enhance the value of I if the item in question is of foreign origin. Some items produced abroad are far superior to Indian goods but certainly not all. For apple, apparel, leatherwear and many more items difference of quality perception between Indian and foreign items is more notional and ad-driven than actual.

We further extend concept of Money (M) from the intermediate Monery (M') to Normey (N), the third beacon, using the following relationship.

$$F'' = (Q_g \cdot V_g) + (Q_a \cdot V_a) + (Q_l \cdot V_l) - (O_g + O_a + O_l)$$
$$= (V_g \cdot R_g / I_g) + (V_a \cdot R_a / I_a) + (V_l \cdot R_l / I_l) - (O_g + O_a + O_l)$$
$$O = w + i + c + d$$
$$F'' - F = (Q_a \cdot V_a) + (Q_l \cdot V_l) - (O_a + O_l)$$
$$q' = (F'' - F)/F = (F''/F) - 1.$$

Thus, Quiddity (Q) relates to market RoE (R) as well as to the absolute carrier of value, Normey (N) by retro-cognition from F". Q and R, two apparently incongruous elements, unite in common embrace of Insipidity Coefficient (I), a factor of profound import.

Economy consists of structure and flow — the latter is in the care of Money. Often, Money is found lacking in its assigned role. So the need for a superior replacement arises. Normey is a plausible candidate in that role. Knowledge of the Normey content of an economy or at least its periodic inflow rate into the economy offers newer perspectives from which to look at the economy, sharper insight with which to analyze the ills that affect the economy and more accuracy in solutions to problems that besiege the economy. Most of all, it allows one the opportunity to set up a Paradigm from rudiments.

Normey is much more comprehensive, inclusive and archetypal than Money. By having Agriculture and Labour drawn into its conceptual fold as elements, Normey affords a panoramic vision of economy much wider than Money does — the latter focused entirely on passage into economy through factory production coupled with exchanges.

Exponents of Money, as such, conveniently ignore occurrences elsewhere in the economy treating them as enigmatic dark spots of no consequence. Their flawed readings leave them clueless when crises erupt. Oblivious of their own one-eyed stance, they allow unaddressed minor issues to pile heedless of rumblings as they occur until these fulminate as implosion leaving the economy rudderless and steeped in major crises. Normey raises hopes of having origins of periodical crises well-covered to probable dislike of protagonists of status quo.

Capitalists are wary of new ideas as they are wont to balance possible losses they might have to incur with adoption of such ideas against the gains. As such gains are *a priori* Capitalists' fear of losing out prevails.

P.68

Normey is an option of looking ahead in a world where stagnation is the order of the day. Unless people's interests enter the calculations with which Capitalists are guided - which is possible by embracing Normey – there is not much to look forward to.

UGLY MONEY, FAIR MONEY

CHAPTER ~ 7 ~

Ugly Money, Fair Money

If Money is ugly because it is upshot of Pricing, the dirty game, then Normey is a game changer, and, being committed to innate value and inclusiveness, is fair and a right element for Paradigm.

Normey-pool, not Money-pool, is the real accumulator of total Wealth. Normey lives unobtrusively in the shadows of Money. It is a reckoner of genuine productive human efforts in amenable form, as endless as an ocean.

Normey, once created, lasts eternally as an ever-widening expanse. It does not deplete by destruction, consumption or anything else. Human efforts in creating Normey need aides that range from none to animals, from ordinary to complex machines and organizations. Normey embodies genuine human effort more aptly and fully than any other reckoner.

Normey does not have a usage aspect though. Taking U as Degree of Unfairness in Pricing, Normey(N) relates to Money(M) as

$$U = M / N$$

assuming that identical mathematical relations prevail between Fresh-inflow of Money (F) and Money-pool (M) on one hand and Fresh-inflow of Normey(F") and Normey-pool (N) on the other, inasmuch as accumulated Money and Normey are similarly apt to create push for Fresh-inflow of Money and Normey respectively.

Money is a concept that treats Factory Production as the heart of Economy while marginalizing Labour and Agriculture by placing them in auxiliary, supporting and external roles. People associated with Core Economy get the prerogative of complete, close and subjective attention while those in Peripheral Economy are treated in distant and objective manner, the attitude inevitably verging on neglect.

If Money is the sheen of the fiber of Economy then Normey is its tensile strength. The role of Money or Normey in Economy is not merely to facilitate exchange, storage and accounting. The real role of both lies in making exchange as it should be that is, setting stringent norms for equitability. Storage and Accounting follows suit. The fiber of Economy should be receptacle of dream of every human being, not merely of those flaunting the rich tag.

Money is incapable of playing such role as it is one-sided, partial and heavily loaded in favour of Factory Production at the expense of Labour and Agriculture. Money is inequitable *ab initio*. It makes some people rich but cannot ensure even a decent living for everyman.

Creation of a few super-rich by consigning vast number of others to abject poverty cannot be a good advertisement by any norms – moral, ethical or pragmatic. It is bound to be a prescription for disaster, sooner or later. In spite of this inglorious part played by Money it cannot be discarded altogether as an unit of conceptualization because of its very strong Usage roots. Rather, Money should strictly be restricted to its Usage role. For other roles namely, Pricing, Storage and Accounting we should look to Normey instead.

Normey is an attempt to make up for the deficiencies in-built in Money. It is designed to redress those aspects for which Money is notorious. It has the right ingredients to be representative of People's dream. Its incisive analytical ways set right the Exchange or, Price.

It transpires that Exchange, or, Price is the single most crucial decider in the running turf war between ninety percent of people who are poverty-stricken and remaining ten percent of rich.

Normey follows certain laws that arise from its inclusive and comprehensive nature that Money lacks, as outlined below.

Law 1 : Normey is created by people's concerted productive efforts. Once created, it cannot be destroyed.

It is a repository of sum total of productive efforts against ongoing time. It supports people in their dreams and aspirations. It is cumulative. Neither consumption nor exchange reduces Normey. It goes on increasing forever.

Law 2 : Absolute volume of accumulation of Normey is beyond measurability and inconsequential too, only its rate of increase over time is measurable and relevant for all practical purposes.

Total volume of Normey is like vastness of ocean measuring which is pointless and impossible too due to paucity of antecedent data. It is an academic exercise, very large in dimension but low on utility.

Law 3 : High concentration of Normey or, richness at one point of economy causes dilution or, poverty at some other point. These two balance each other out about the ruling average of Normey.

If the two points are part of the same and closed economy, then there would be as much poverty at one point as there would be richness at the other. If the points are part of two different economies interconnected by foreign trade then one country would be a rich country while the other would be poor.

Law 4 : Creation of Fresh-inflow of Normey into a Normey-pool is proportional to the size of the Normey-pool in the short-term during tenancy of which Productive-apparatus is unchanged.

Productive-apparatus includes technology, people's taste and product-revolution. The maxim of possession, excluding gifting, is that one has to buy a thing by spending for it in order to possess it, which includes Productive-apparatus. As size of Normey-pool increases, availability, affordability and acquiring of productive-apparatus becomes easier. As Productive-apparatus gains strength it facilitates higher production and larger Fresh-inflow of Normey.

It transpires that as time moves on and as cycles come one after another Normey-pool enlarges continuously, without interruption and in the same direction that is, without negative growth. It is also an important corollary of this law that growth in the size of Normey pool actually accelerates – it does not merely grow at a steady pace. The reason is that growth rate is proportional to size and size increases unabatedly.

Law 5 : In the short-term, Fresh-creation of Normey bears an identical relationship to Volume of Normey-pool as does Fresh-creation of Money to Volume of Money-pool.

If Fresh-creation of Money is related to Volume of Money-pool through intervention of a proportionality constant then the same proportionality constant relates Fresh-creation of Normey to Volume of Normey-pool. It transpires that, in the short-term,

$$U = F / F''$$
$$\text{or, } U = ((Q_g \cdot V_g) - O_g) / ((Q_g \cdot V_g) + (Q_a \cdot V_a) + (Q_l \cdot V_l) - (O_g + O_a + O_l)).$$

As all the quantities on the right are derivable from observation and by approximation, we can measure U. In turn, from M we get N. Knowledge of Normey equivalent of Money puts one in a position of strength to argue the case of deprivation and lack of fairness of Price.

Increasing vastness of Normey compels humanity to stretch its imagination to find ever newer ways of deploying it to fruitful endeavours. Such compulsion often lead to inferior choices of deployment. However, Normey, by its very design, does not allow Toxicity an entry into the treasury of the Normey-pool. While in case of Money a sizable bulk goes to building Toxicity, in case of Normey the undeployable bulk is likely to remain just idle.

Tenability is an indicator of appropriateness of deployment as to its chance of success, wholesomeness and judiciousness. It is apt as a policy-aide too.

Absolute Tenability (T_n) =
(Quantum of Normey appropriately deployed) /
(Quantum of actual accumulated total Normey).

Since actual accumulated total Normey is beyond measurability, the idea of Absolute Tenability is of limited and academic interest.

Relative Tenability (T_n) is a more pragmatic concept because of its intimate association with live data.

Relative Tenability (T_n) =
(Quantum of appropriate deployment fraction of Normey in current year)/
(Quantum of appropriate deployment fraction of Normey in the year 2000 AD).

If N_{2K} is quantum of total Normey in 2000 AD, N_{a2K} is quantum of appropriate deployment of Normey in 2000 AD and g is current growth of Normey with reference to 2000 AD as the base year, we have,

$$T_n = ((1/N_{2K}) \cdot (N_a/(1+g)))/ ((1/N_{2K}) \cdot N_{a2K})$$
$$= (N_a/(1+g))/ N_{a2K}.$$

Relative Tenability (T_n) is also of limited utility since it does not reveal deviation, if any, from the ideal mean or the extent of such deviation.

Tenability Trend (T_t), the most useful indicator of deployment of Normey, being trend-related, is ratio of short-term to long-term trends.

Tenability Trend (T_t) =

(Average of year-wise appropriate deployment fractions of Normey in last 3 years)/

(Average of year-wise appropriate deployment fractions of Normey since 2000 AD).

or, T_t = $SUM_j\ ((1/N_{2K}) \cdot (N_{aj}/(1+g_j)))/ SUM_i\ ((1/N_{2K}) \cdot (N_{ai}/(1+g_i)))$

= $SUM_j\ (N_{aj}/(1+g_j))/ SUM_i\ (N_{ai}/(1+g_i))$

where i ranges from 2000 AD to current year and j is 1,2,3 from now backwards. Weakly positive T_t is cause for concern. Negative T_t is alarming, needing immediate measures to reverse the trend.

UGLY MONEY, FAIR MONEY

Chapter ~ 8 ~

Money-making Marks : Bias, Cast, Drift, Edge and Hyperform

Mobility of Money leads to Money accumulation and opens the Pandora's Box called Money-making. It is part of the Capitalist process[3], sequel to skewed Pricing and no less vicious an aspect of Capitalism than Pricing is. It has Marks to capture sole and mass degree of vilification. The Need to curtail wanton Money-making, as the Money-spinner cleverly wields his deadly weapon, brand, in uneven contest, finds embodiment in Policy. Mentally mutated consumers favour big brands over less illustrious and labour-intensive Small Scale Industry (SSI) units when bigs with capital-intensive capacity/technology vie with SSI for vast markets of salt, soap, cereals, fruit etc in hugely populated India. Consumer apathy helps the bigs who create a few jobs but destroy myriad others. Their Cost Pattern reveals a few leads.

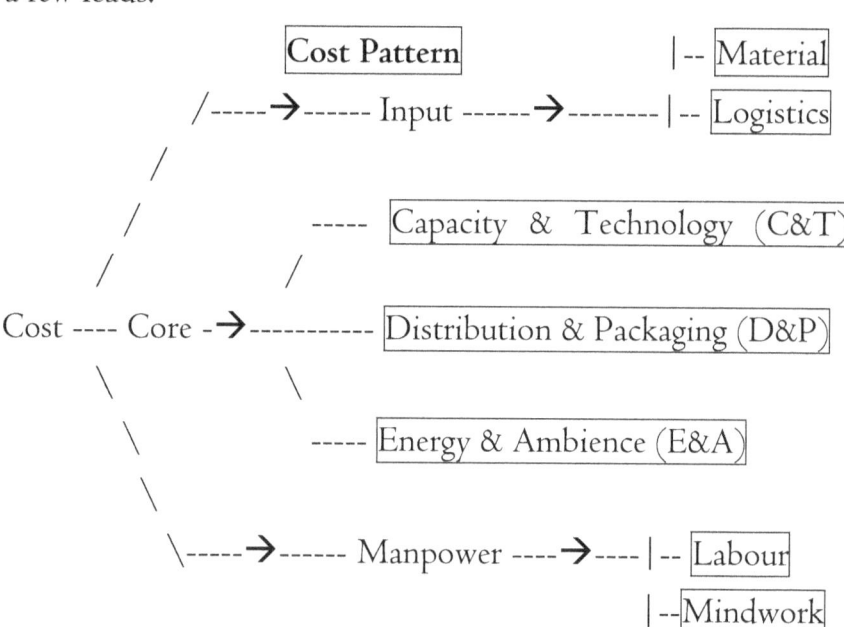

Core Cost is gradual acquisition of C&T along with D&P and E&A set-ups. Manpower is physical Labour, Skill and Mind application.

3 J. A. Schumpeter, "Capitalism, Socialism & Democracy", p140

Bias (B_i) is outcrop of relation between Core cost and Total cost over time. It differentiates minnows SSIs from big players. Rising Bias, typical of a non-SSI, boosts its productivity as SSI Bias and productivity stay immobile.

$$\text{Bias } (B_i) = \text{Rate of change of (Core cost/ Total cost)}$$
$$\text{Cast } (C_a) = (\text{Aggregate Bias}) + 20 . (\text{Economic Growth Rate}).$$

B_i has the ideal value 1 when production mode is balanced. $B_i < 1$ is labour intensive, $B_i > 1$ is labour deficient. For entire economy, C_a has range 0-1 for IE, 1 < range < 5 for UE and range 5-5+ for LE.

Bias (Bi), extended to policy, has profound implications. In labour intensive economy consumers get enhanced net buying power on dispersion of production spoils. A labour deficient economy disperses among fewer recipients causing depletion of net buying power. Joblessness among its citizens does not augur well for economies going all-out for growth. $B_i \gg 1$ gives edge to growth but lacks enough stress on quantum of buying power and its pattern of distribution.

Same aggregate buying power is more effective if shared among larger number of hands. Aggressive all-growth strategy causes loss of urge to buy in the long run, leading to crises of over-production and recession. Afflicted economy then looks desperately to over-populated destinations for relief through export. $B_i \ll 1$ sets top priority on humanism, pruning growth. This policy cannot help pace the economy though. So, $B_i = 1$ is right.

Cast (C_t) is a composite quantity, a feature of the entire economy and an aide that depicts quantum and trend of development of an economy. Efficacy of C_t lies in the fact that besides the growth parameter it contains a variable for mode of achievement of the growth.

In Large Economies (LE), overall C_t is much greater than 1. Drift (D_f) is a numeral directly proportional to C_t and always larger than C_t. D_f rises slowly to approach ($C_t + 1$) as the economy develops except in case of the largest economy that has $D_{f1} = C_{t1} + 1$ always. D_f, also a useful measure of development, parallels C_t.

$$D_f = J + J' \cdot C_t \quad [J, \text{Juxtaposition constant, fixed in short term}]$$
$$\text{or, } D_f = J + C_t \quad\quad\quad\quad [J' = 1 \text{ by assumption}]$$
$$\text{or, } D_{fi} = J_i + C_{ti}.$$

Since J_i is economy specific so would be D_i. We need to assign values to J_i. A reasonable approach would be to derive it from the following stipulation, applicable to all economies, with the Largest Economy having $J_1 = 1$.

$$J_i = (\text{size of i-th economy})/(\text{size of largest economy}).$$

Juxtaposition Constant (J) is indicative of closeness of an economy to the largest economy and varies in the long term. Its variation pattern reveals trend in standing of the economy in the global context. This aspect of global standing is the essential separator between C_t and D_f.

P.81

Edge (E_d), a qualitative measure of development, relates to Fabric (F_b), or organizational bedrock, while Ken (K_e) is on human resources having two parts - one, K_q, is for quality including knowledge and skill and two, K_n, is numeric strength as fraction of global numeric strength. Lead (L_d) is on technological excellence.

$$E_{di} = F_{bx} + (K_{qi} \cdot K_{ni}) + L_d' \cdot L_{di} \quad [L' \text{ is proportionality constant}]$$

E_d is necessary because not all advanced economies are as large as they are advanced while there are very large economies which are not that advanced. Lacking empirical sources, for above method of assessment we use arbitrary values of F_b, K_e and L_d and optimize.

Assuming for technologically the most advanced $L_{da} = I$, in the range 0-I, $F_{da} = I$ for such economy being organizationally most accomplished too, in the range 0-I, and $K_{qa} = I$ in the range 0-I, we get, putting $E_{da} = 1000$ in the scale I-1000,

$$1000 = I + + I \cdot K_{na} + I \cdot L_d'$$
or, $L_d' = 999 - K_{na}$
or, $E_{di} = F_{bx} + (K_{qi} \cdot K_{ni}) + (999 - K_{na}) \cdot L_{di}$.

Hyperform (H_y), reification of idiosyncrasy of an economy, is assorted esse of all developments, quantitative and qualitative.

$$H_{yi} = D_{fi} + E_{di}$$
or, $H_{yi} = C_{ti} + J_i + F_{bx} + (K_{qi} \cdot K_{ni}) + (999 - K_{na}) \cdot L_i$.

Twenty years back, when aggregate B_i began to rise for foodgrains, Govt allowed the trend to continue. Gradually, inaction pushed the RoE level so high that nearly the entire populace was left screaming. Govt responded by increasing dearness allowances but that was hardly the right cure. It was a palliative that left cause of RoE increase unaddressed. Benefit of RoE rise percolated down to the lowest stratum of society – the small farmers – slowly and only in part. Most of the benefit was gobbled up by middlemen. Bias was strongly positive as Govt had to act at the instance of foreign lenders to implement Reform. Production of foodgrains should in general be brought under Protected Production Area (PPA) norm.

Reform was part of the conditions for obtaining loan from foreign lenders. It was a ploy to push the Core/ Labour ratio level up to those prevalent in LE. Priority in Core was implied as it opened the way for entry of stale foreign machinery and technology.

Evidence of shifting Bias (B_i) emits the warning signal that a labour intensive area is going the wrong way, possibly through exploitative encroachment on traditional production practice by vested interests from outside. Govt should step in at the earliest sign of predators becoming active in a protected production area. I also gives us a chance to evaluate labour against a neutral perspective free of the usual distortional influence of market. This is particularly true for labour intensive areas like agriculture and acutely more so where small farmers are both owners of the land and providers of labour in growing the crop.

UGLY MONEY, FAIR MONEY

CHAPTER ~ 9 ~

Money-making : How it Warps the Minds

As we move from Pricing and Money-making to impact of Money-making on minds we dig up more dirt. Money-making, gruesome and profoundly affecting human behavior, combines lethally with Politics in enactment of infirm and loose laws. Thus, inexplicably, RoE of common salt in India rose 10 times in the past 35 years or, roughly, 30 percent per year.

Traditionally, most salt is made in poor coastal areas using primitive technology and no machinery at all. Energy used is sunlight. Input is sea water – free, abundant, needing no logistics. So, the cost is largely of labour with some for distribution. Clearly, this tenfold rise in RoE came from incursion of big players into the field since such rise in manpower cost in the space of 35 years in remote areas is hard to imagine. Inflation rates are far lesser.

New entrants, glib on process superiority, multiple health benefits such as less impurities and more iodine, presented a superb package. Govt hyped in with campaign for iodine content that helped the bigs. Initially, difference was a trifling 3 to 4 Rs/kg. Consumers, oblivious of the fact that in the process they were depriving lakhs of poor people of their livelihood from salt, fell for it. The goodness radiated by branded salt was more made up than real.

With consumers in their grip bigs went on raising RoE with impunity. Despite minimal quality difference, salt with low labour content won over high labour content. Consumers, bothered, if at all, not by cruel stifling of ethos but by health-scare, gladly paid tenfold more letting opportunists to exploit mass gullibility.

P.85

This cunning mindplay can be made stingless by Govt intervention in the form of protective taxation, declaring salt a Protected Production Area (PPA). Thus if traditional producers of salt are charged with 2 percent tax branded producers would pay tax at 20 percent rate.

It would be an eminently justified step as moneyed people cannot be allowed to make more money pushing the poor salt makers to starvation. Govt outlets would sell salt at Rs 5 per kg. Govt would campaign for the traditional salt asserting its merits such as drying in the sun for days that kills all germs and that sea water already contains enough iodide for normal needs. Govt should also tell people that only a miniscule part of the population is affected by medical conditions arising out of dearth of iodine. This will create a level playing field. All cost-wary sensible consumers could revert back to traditional salt while others would stay with branded salt even paying 10 times more.

Empathy towards the poor is cruel joke. So, RoE of wheat, staple food of bulk of all Indians including the poor, is allowed to grow 300 percent over 20 years, enhancing the inflation spiral, which works out to be 15 percent per year. This steep upward trend was triggered by entry of big commercial houses in trade of packaged wheat products and other packaged agricultural items.

The difference largely enters their pockets and they make huge profits without value addition except in packaging. Big commercial houses use agricultural brand handle to make a neat kill. As ever, Labour, largest contributor to wheat growing, remains sidelined. As Core cost soars and as Labour cost remains static B also soars.

Repressed urge of B_i to gather momentum to rise in value leads to perversion. Perversion breeds corruption which percolates down to the lowest levels. More the underdevelopment, more are the chances of perversion and corruption.

Fishing in troubled waters is the politician's age-old practice. While delivering platitudes and commiserating with the poor they shape up as the hare, as if ready to run with other hares. While seeing nails being driven into coffin of fairness they unabashedly hunt with the hound.

Politics presents the ruler with the crucial escape-hatch without which the ruler would get trapped by its own laws. Politics gives immunity to those in power and compensates this laxity by being more severe to the commoner. Politics is the stage where the ruler appears in guise of constructive role player to defuse strife and help ruler achieve his ends.

Politics in UE, besides playing the designated role of governance, positions itself as the interventionist and prevents perversion from surfacing through diabolical, often the meanest of, means together with rhetoric in which patriotism coupled with mud-slinging take lead part. In fact, in politics in UE, governance becomes secondary to perversion-management with payment of covert fees. People engaged in politics in UE wear multiple disposable masks, one at a time. There is no place for morality in politics in UE as morality is a part of truth.

Politics in LE, riding a different set of variables, copes with problems as associated with other extreme of the spectrum. Checking rampant rise in B_i also gives rise to corruption but of an unlike kind.

Viciousness is the hallmark of the ruler mindset in the present day. The seeds that gave rise to such a ugly outgrowth were laid long before the advent of the current age with the ingraining of two patently base concepts into the mass mindset which is lacerating deep into the mass scruple ever since. The first of these is speculation associated with trading of shares in the secondary share market (SSM) which is akin to gambling. Actually, it is a far cry from genuine investment in production of goods.

Second in line is the theme of intermediation of which differential interests – the main banking mantra – is the core. Bank gains huge amounts doing nothing and shares some of its gains with the actual owners of the funds. Bank takes risk and comes, in the process, to the assistance of millions of helpless people such as the old and the infirm who have some money but cannot deploy it by themselves in work.

Turning a blind eye to potentially irreparable damage likely to be caused by it to moral fabric of people is like smugly allowing spread of cancerous cells till the day of reckoning when a great implosion takes care of it all. Its positive sides notwithstanding, a nation dominated by glorified gamblers and polished pawnbrokers joining in a split personality cannot be sweet reflection, however one looks at it.

With a corrupt moral fabric we cannot hope to look far ahead beyond the immediate. The tragic side of it is that SSM and banking are both bulwarks of the Capitalist system without which the system cannot exist. Neither SSM nor banking can get rid of the debauchery that mark their respective area of activity.

Capitalist system is a curious recipe of exciting and obnoxious features. One has to take it as a whole or leave it altogether. The parts are so intimately inter-connected that selectively opting out of some of them only cripples the system. The parts are inseparably linked in a single mass. So, in a Capitalist system one has to live with such incongruities.

Democracy is a garb of convenience to convey verisimilitude of concern about people's woes and eagerness to redress those while actually and surreptitiously aiding Capitalist menagerie to achieve its ends. A democratic republic is no different from an autocratic republic or a monarchy in this regard, except for directness of the last two.

There is hope nevertheless. Some of the core concepts can be supplemented with judicious application of logic. One such area is Pricing, which is the mechanism for creating Money. Going deep into the mechanism itself, it is possible to overhaul Pricing. Money will follow suit obviating the necessity to change it.

The flawed and rotten areas of Pricing that makes it heavily biased in favour of the ruler can be selectively addressed and ruthlessly removed. This practice has a long history dating back to start of Capitalism two hundred years age. It is not necessary that it should last forever.

One possible alternative approach is to maintain the Usage aspect of Money as it is now but let Normey be sourced for policy all matters. Such equation will balance the system without toppling it. In order to make this procedure feasible, constant track of the Unfairness factor, relating the two, has to be kept. As the rules change so will the rulers.

Invidious intrigue that mark Pricing and Money-making leaves its evil imprint on people's minds too. Capitalist System recognizes only entities useful to its propagation and reinforcement. To others, it offers heartless indifference. It idolizes excellence and treats the ordinary with ungracious rebuff.

The mind is mind – it reacts and adapts in its own way. People lose faith in a System that does not care for the weak under its fold. It becomes a System of the privileged, by the privileged and for the privileged. In spite of reaction to rebuff, race to earn foothold in life continues unabated turning social relationships hollow.

The reaction, soft or hard, often turns to extremes - to malignancy but of different kinds. Unpredictability of the mind precludes charting the direction a particular mind might take or statistically indicating movement of mass psyche. Logic loses out to passion, preempting sane intervention. Broadly, there are three types of affectations.

Dip is distrust in common ruled minds coming as an unwanted gift from the System. Dip also raises simmering rage in the mind.

Dent is quirk caused to the mind by the System. Dent makes the mind insensitive and reclusive too.

Despair comes from a System unsupportive to the weak. Down and out people often turn to extreme modes. Cowering is the likely choice else, attacking the System - sometimes engaging in bloody internal warfare.

Those who cower but do not succeed in climbing the high wall of ordeals carefully erected by the System to sift out the best are left in dire straits in which etching out a decent livelihood – one of dignity, hope and care – becomes a distant dream.

This type is by far the largest in number. They are docile on the surface but inside each of them rage boils. They are drawn to obscurantist practices for courage to cope with adversity as the System is perceived as being hostile. To them God is the savior because they need a savior – whether God exists or not is a question they do not ask or desist from seeking an answer to it in earnest. Curiously, their hope lies in their rage – that someday many such rages would come out in the open and join forces to slay the demon, the heartless System.

The origin of it all lies in the unavoidable aspect of how the System deals with the non-excellent people – the average. The System that does not own up responsibility of accommodating bulk of the populace in its folds other than merely using them as buyers of products produced and sold by its production and distribution apparatus is destined to be a failure in contenting people in general. Regrettably, Capitalists do not aim at all to make people content.

The question of how Money-making might possibly be involved in mass psychic distortion is to be examined now. The Capitalist dogma revolves around production-sale-Money generation. Such is the intensity with which this routine is enacted that any other factor that disturbs the routine with loss of rhythm – a critical aspect of far reaching consequences inviting exceptional rigidity – is ignored.

In other words, the Capitalist juggernaut ruthlessly crushes under its wheels thoughts, ideas, views, protests, non-conformist beliefs, demand for rights that run contrary to its course. There is no reasoned elaboration why a communist deserves to be killed merely because he is a communist. The alacrity with which this dictum was once practiced in the Capitalist parts of the world during the heydays of socialism that the dictum came to be elevated to the high level of truism.

Thus Money-making under Capitalism is regarded as the holiest of holy thoughts from which no deviation is tolerated. If anybody asks why Money-making should take the place of one's soul and the soul relegated to an inferior and innocuous subsidiary role he is branded a heretic communist. Since fall of the socialist bloc, a milder epithet, leftist, is also used to describe such people as they are now fangless, much to the relief of the Capitalists.

Without confining thoughts in a cramped space with limited leeway and by allowing antagonism a free run Capitalism cannot survive for long. So, the mass mind is perforce put under straitjacket under Capitalism. This use of straitjacket over minds is the root cause of all afflictions that the minds have to cope with in Capitalism.

The difficulty of existing with a free-thinking mind yet keeping in pursuit of glory is just not possible under Capitalism because the prerogatives that the system have to be regarded as solemn and any line of contra-thinking cannot be allowed to flourish unless it subjugates itself to the system prerogatives.

Unless the mind is free it cannot bring in fresh ideas that help expand the horizons of life. Technological breakthrough cannot take the place of mental amelioration. Attempts to treat cancer with drugs for diabetes invariably ends up in failure. The fault does not lie in drug selection but in the desperation that takes the place of sanity when there is no drug to treat cancer with.

With growing impoverishment of the mind - that inexorably comes with advancement of Capitalism – being the affliction, introduction of superior technology as in high-end android phone can hardly be the right medication. Instead of rise in the number of mentally superior human beings what we get is plethora of mean human beings rolling in opulence but extremely well adapted to the use of technology and a deplorable dearth of the type of man with lofty ideals, broad visions and wide intellectual reach - to have whom among a group of people would make the group proud.

The crux of the matter is that the Capitalist dispensation prescribes and hands out to common people palliative medications and cosmetic surgery for ailments lying deep inside the core of human relations. Occasional volcanic eruptions are only to be expected from such a state of inconsistency. Actually, Capitalists have no other option for, otherwise, their own existence could be at stake.

UGLY MONEY, FAIR MONEY

C*HAPTER* ~ 10 ~

Normey : Fair Visage of Money, Vehicle of People's Dream

Ultimately, it is the people and their dreams that matter. Egregious Pricing, its upshot - Money, along with Money-making corrode the fabric of People's dream. It is Normey that really carries people's dream forward. Money allures and encourages desperation, often luring astray towards the impossible and, not unusually, to ruin. Normey reflects the true reality and gives one courage to march on, that comes from exact knowledge of facts regarding thorns, pitfalls and dangers en route to achievement besides clarity about one's own merits and limitations. Certainty breeds confidence.

In a world where disparity of wealth distribution rules and grows starkly every day, it is no wisdom to go by what Money advises. The route indicated by Money would leave the poor poorer and more numerous while the rich richer and fewer, percentage-wise. A point is reached where every poor has to take up the cudgels against unfairness. He gets Normey by his side. When the system is extremely reluctant to pass on the fair dues of an Effective Producer (EP) to him, he finds the courage to fight the system for his dues — emboldened by veracious exposition of Normey.

Pricing should be based on Normey. Once the fair Wage of an EP is determined in terms of Normey it can be easily translated to Money. The EP can then press for fair Wage using hard evidence.

Equitable distribution of gains from production would certainly lead to a more egalitarian society. It is not necessary that talents would stand to lose recognition in such a scenario. It all depends on the system to make certain that it does not happen.

Such a scenario sounds as mere conjecture in the present circumstances. The entire Capitalist Fraternity (CF) including the paid thinktank is expected to oppose any move towards implementation of such ideas as their very over-glorified existence will be threatened by introduction of fairness in Dispersion Arrangement (DA). As the academic circles cherish and propagate their own pernicious and bigoted thinking process, it is extremely difficult for such notions - regarded by one and all in their ranks as outlandish and heretic - even to trickle in among young minds.

In trying to find a precise mathematical entity to represent fairness we have to go back and get to the following equation

$$N = (1/U) \cdot M$$

where U is the Degree of Unfairness which tells us that in order to find the Normey equivalent of a quantum of Money we need to multiply the quantum by a factor $1/U$. So, $1/U$ is Degree of Fairness which is usually greater than 1 with lowest possible value of 1. Expanding further, we get,

$$1/U = ((Q_g \cdot V_g) + (Q_a \cdot V_a) + (Q_1 \cdot V_1) - (O_g + O_a + O_1))/((Q_g \cdot V_g) - O_g)$$

or, $1/U = 1 + ((Q_a \cdot V_a) + (Q_1 \cdot V_1) - (O_a + O_1))/((Q_g \cdot V_g) - O_g)$.

Clearly, as from the above, under condition of downright unfairness as in slavery and serfdom, marked as Acceptability Level Negative First (ALI-),

$$(Q_a \cdot V_a) + (Q_l \cdot V_l) - (O_a + O_l)) = 0.$$

In slightly better conditions, as in the present day Capitalist system, Acceptability Level Nil (AL0),

$$1 > (Q_a \cdot V_a) + (Q_l \cdot V_l) - (O_a + O_l))/ ((Q_g \cdot V_g) - O_g) > 0.$$

At the First Level of Acceptability (AL1),

$$(Q_a \cdot V_a) + (Q_l \cdot V_l) - (O_a + O_l))/ ((Q_g \cdot V_g) - O_g) = 1.$$

At the Second Level of Acceptability (AL2), which is favoured,

$$(Q_a \cdot V_a) + (Q_l \cdot V_l) - (O_a + O_l)) = 2 \cdot ((Q_g \cdot V_g) - O_g).$$

At AL1, the recognized contributions to total production of Agriculture and Labour combined equal that of Manufacturing of Goods. Pricing has to be done accordingly. As such, at AL1,

$$I/U = I + ((Q_a \cdot V_a) + (Q_l \cdot V_l) - (O_a + O_l))/ ((Q_g \cdot V_g) - O_g))$$

or, $I/U = I + I = 2$

or, $U = 0.50$.

At levels of acceptability higher than AL1, $U < 0.5$. By similar logic, at AL2, we have $I/U = 3$ and $U = 0.33$.

Now, $U = F / F"$.

At AL1, then, $F" = 2F$. That is, the Fresh-creation of Normey is twice the Fresh creation of Money.

At AL1, then, $F" = 3F$. That is, the Fresh-creation of Normey is thrice the Fresh-creation of Money. The Ideal Level of Acceptability (ILA), AL2i is a special case of AL2 where,

$$(Q_a \cdot V_a) - O_a = (Q_l \cdot V_l) - O_l = (Q_g \cdot V_g) - O_g.$$

Any level higher than AL2 may not be viable though, from the point of its sustainability under a Capitalist dispensation.

ILA has an extraordinary significance in the context of people's dreams. Dream associated with aspiration are basically of two types. One, dream of the rich and the powerful few who are keen on holding on to their opulence as also to further enlarge it for the sake of enlarging. These people would like to see fairness level of AL1-implemented, only if they have their ways.

Two, dream of the very large majority of multitude of the poor and the underprivileged who do not have access to basic necessities of life but want to live decent lives. They would look eagerly to the day when their labour gets fairly rewarded. They like to see fairness level AL2i implemented.

What kind of dream would be the policy-maker's pick? Hardliners with the AL1- orientation have since softened their stand, settling for AL0 instead. Following creation of USSR and the Great Depression of 1929-35 US President Roosevelt set in motion certain adaptive practices, cosmetic though they were, to attune the mindset of his citizens to the new reality in the form of his New Deal. He borrowed liberally from Karl Marx's The Communist Manifesto, written in 1848, as to social aspects contained in his New Deal for pragmatic tempering of and toning down on their bullyist doctrine to become humane. What he did was to put seal of largest Capitalist nation on the shift from AL1- to AL0, a rare historic landmark. Roosevelt completed what Lincoln had started.

Among right thinking and fair minded people who abhor bullying and slave-driving in any form as well as subjugating of talents to such abominable forms of humanity the right kind of dream is of course dream type two, because it carries the interests of hundreds of millions of human beings instead of that of a selective few that dream type one does. After all, wealth is for serving humanity seeking to meet its necessities, not for gratifying desires of grotesque minds, a small fraction of humanity, for acquiring unseemly pile of possessions and reveling in luxury. Primeness of such objective need to be established by snatching the initiative from the perverted practitioners of wealth amassment. That does not come easily. But once this maxim is ingrained in the thought process of the majority and temptation to side with the rich and the powerful for a pittance is resisted, AL2i cannot be far away.

www.ingramcontent.com/pod-product-compliance
Lightning Source LLC
Chambersburg PA
CBHW020546220526
45463CB00006B/2212